RETURN TO EDEN

RETURN TO EDEN

by Frederick A. Drummond, Sr.

Destiny Ministries International Church

Return to Eden

Published by
DESTINY MINISTRIES INTERNATIONAL CHURCH

First Printing 2016
Printed in Canada
ISBN: 978-0-692-81032-3

CREDITS

All quoted excerpts from human sources in this book were chosen at face value for their important contribution to this author's premise, and they are gratefully appreciated. Their acceptance, however, does not necessarily represent complete endorsement of every author's other opinions or views expressed in their various works; nor does it imply that inclusion of these quotes constitutes their support for everything stated in this book. Listed below are special credits or acknowledgements for some of these sources.

CONTENTS

ACKNOWLEDGMENTS

I would like to thank all those who helped me to complete this work.

I am fortunate enough to have a wife, Lorraine, who is perfectly suited to help me in my work. No matter what time of day or night I have called on her to write something down or look something up, she has been more than willing to do so with a sweet spirit. I also need to mention my two sons, Frederick and David, whose contribution has been indispensable.

For more than three decades Randall Vinson has helped me with my research and endlessly edited everything I have written. He is a gift from heaven, a dear friend, and a true Bible student.

Many have sacrificed their time to help me in spite of their own busy schedules. To all I say thank you. I would like to mention Richard Price, and especially Grace Bellingham for broadening my perspective with her down-to-earth suggestions and her tireless reading of my manuscripts.

Most of all, the credit goes to the Holy Spirit Who has been my constant companion and Friend through it all since 1965. Truly He has convinced me over and over again that His grace is sufficient, and that to live by love is to live like God.

FAD, Sr.

INTRODUCTION

The new creation is outrageous. It is the answer you have been looking for all your life. Nothing can beat what it offers. It is clearly the fulfillment of prophecies God has made from the beginning. It not only solves the dilemma created by the fall in the Garden of Eden so many years ago, but it does so in ways that no one ever expected. Who would have thought that there would be a second Adam and a second creation? It came as a surprise to all. Not even those Jews who were watching for their Messiah imagined such things.

From the earliest mention, the glories about Christ and His new creation that would populate new heavens and a new earth were shrouded in prophecies, allegories, promises, experiences, and psalms they sang that didn't fully reveal the glory that was yet to come. The Holy Bible speaks of the mystery of Christ as veiled. Until God revealed it to the apostles, its meaning remained at best guesswork. Not even the angels could figure it out.

> Of this salvation the prophets have inquired and searched carefully, who prophesied of the grace that would come to you,
> searching what, or what manner of time, the Spirit of Christ who was in them was indicating when He testified beforehand the sufferings of Christ and the glories that would follow.
> To them it was revealed that, not to themselves, but to us they were ministering the things which now have been reported to you through those who have preached the gospel to you by the Holy Spirit sent from heaven—things which angels desire to look into.
> Therefore gird up the loins of your mind, be sober, and rest your hope fully upon the grace that is to be brought to you at the revelation of Jesus Christ;
>
> *1 Pet. 1:10–13*

Certainly no one ever expected a second creation; nevertheless, this is precisely what God always had on His mind from the beginning. For that matter, neither did anyone expect a second Adam to birth that new creation, but that is how the Holy Scriptures describe Jesus and His mission (1 Cor. 15:45,47; Rom. 8:29; Eph. 1:3–12).

In order to better grasp the magnitude of the new creation message, we ought to avoid flattening out the message of the cross to its simplest form—forgiveness of sins. The coming of Christ had a far bigger view of God's intentions than that. Don't get me wrong, thank God for forgiveness.

The guilty couldn't hear anything more beautiful than "I forgive you, and I will never remember or bring up your sins again." Feast on this, Christian. Enjoy it! This is what Jesus accomplished on the cross for you. No religion has ever come up with anything so generous. But don't stop there. Move on and see how much more God has done for you—He has birthed a new creation, and you are a part of it. What does this all mean?

Jesus came to put right everything that has gone wrong in the world since satan became its god at the fall (1 John 3:8). It is exciting to me to know that I as a Christian am a part of the second Adam's new creation that will live forever in newness, exploring the pleasures of God forevermore. Nothing can top that! No one can offer you more. Christian, this is God's best for you. No wonder the Scriptures speak of it as "so great a salvation" (Heb. 2:3).

Fortunately, the good news about a second Adam and His second creation born of the Spirit isn't just about tomorrow after the resurrection in the end. It is also about today and the amazing life that is ours as we get to enjoy every blessing in heaven in Christ through grace.

New words have been added to our vocabulary as new creation believers. While they have all been mentioned in the Scriptures before, today they have gained fresh, new meaning that we will explore together in this book. For example, the word "faith." God's people have always lived by faith, and yet today believers have the faith of God (Mark 11:22) to perform the impossible. Then there is the word "grace" that means so much more to us today because it governs this dispensation and sets us free as believers to reign in life powerfully (Rom. 5:17). What about the word "forgive," knowing God will never remember our sins again; and the word "love" and how it is shed abroad in our hearts by the Spirit to show off what heaven on earth looks like? Then there are words like "freedom" and "hope" and "church," etc., all of which have taken on new meanings for Christ's new creation.

If there was a first Eden where God walked with man, enjoying communion together as they practiced their new-found dominion over everything, then there is also with the second Adam and His new creation a second Eden that will yet fill new heavens and a new earth that we get to enjoy in part today in our churches.

I have written this book to inspire you to rediscover your faith. I want you to fall in love with God all over again and recognize the grand possibilities that are yours today to live out the dreams-come-true life that He has planned for you. This is an inspirational book to ignite hope in your heart (Rom. 15:13). It is His story.

Get excited. My message is "Show off your newness," and "Beat the old world at their game with the new world's answers." Christ's new creation knows how to live. Jesus called it a more abundant life (John 10:10), and the writer of the book of Hebrews said that we get to enjoy better promises today than God has ever made to anyone (Heb. 8:6). God has spoiled His new creation in the best sense of the word. They are fat with His blessings, rich through His promises, and strong through His might and power—they have it made, they know Him personally, and they will live forever.

FAD, Sr.

CHAPTER 1

The Need to Return to Eden

A Beginning

God loved Eden and made it a special place where He could share Himself with His beloved creation, mankind. It was a perfect place where they could enjoy one another and know nothing but love. It was a place of dreams and peace where harmony, pleasure, and superabundance prevailed. God and man were one in love.

Returning to Eden's love isn't just a good idea; it is a necessity. If man is ever to be restored to a relationship with God, he is going to have to come to grips with the sublime truth that God in all His holiness is love. For us to return to fellowship with Him we must be restored to that love. Therein lies the story of redemption and the pathway God has laid out for man to take to empower him for this journey.

We believers have this love birthed in us by the Spirit in preparation for that happy day when we hear the trumpet sound and are totally absorbed into God's new world of love, a perfect, new creation never to be lost again. I am getting ahead of myself in saying these things, but this is a good place to start in explaining the need to return to Eden and enjoy the personal relationship with God that His love demands. Let us go back to the beginning where this was lost in the Garden of Eden so long ago, and see how God has remedied it all for us through Jesus Christ the second Adam, and His amazing grace.

It was out of the overflow of His boundless love that He made man in His own image to be included in the love that has always existed between the Father, Son, and Holy Spirit. This amazing beginning is hard to grasp; nevertheless, it is true. Stanley J. Grenz points out that this "act of creation arises out of God's love.…God is love—a love manifest between the Father, Son, and Holy Spirit. The act of creation, in turn, is the 'outflowing' of this eternal love relationship within the heart of God."[1] Why He would create something out of nothing and love that something so much that He would invite it to join in the Triune fellowship of love that has always existed, none of us will ever be able to figure out. There is no understanding this kind of "unconstrained love," as Colin E. Gunton calls it.[2] "God's love knows no *why* beyond itself—there is no reason for God's love apart from his love," wrote Thomas F. Torrance;[3] and in the words of Gerald Bray, "Love is its own explanation, because God is love."[4] As we can see, then, it must be accepted and embraced by faith because there is no example of it anywhere on earth. And yet this loving invitation is precisely what God had in mind when He made Adam and Eve. He loved them and wanted them, and He foresaw a multitude of men and women being born out of the holy union that they shared together.

Nothing like this had ever been done before. Yet when everything was ready, man was made a little lower than the angels, not because he meant less to God or they were better than he was; in fact, the opposite was true. God did so to contain man in time while He prepared everything for eternity on this earth.

Angels are important. They are God's ministers (servants) who do His will—magnificent beings with supernatural power, designed to worship God and help the redeemed on their journey of life (Heb. 1:13,14). We, on the other hand, are His offspring. What a phenomenon of grace. We have been destined to become one with Him forever on this planet—a part of the divine Family of Three. No one should question that we are more important and closer to God than anything else that He has created (Acts 17:28,29); in fact, in the words of Robert Letham, we are "the crown of his creation, representing him as his image bearers."[5]

When you take a step back and consider the Garden of Eden in the scheme of things, its important role is realized and its prophetic nature comes to light—it foreshadowed man's destiny to live in unbroken fellowship with God. It was the perfect environment of love that we were designed to thrive in forever with Him (Gen. 1:26–28), and there is no improving this. As Gregory A. Boyd states, "[W]e were created for unbroken, loving fellowship with God…to have his perfect, triune love displayed to us, in us, and through us."[6] And Torrance tells us that God "made us for fellowship with himself in order to share with us his divine Life and Light and Love."[7]

None of today's problems existed in that garden, nor could they have. We live in a lesser world today, one that is contrary to us, whether we realize it or not. Our world is eaten up by the degenerative influence of judgmentalism, fear, and death, longing for the superabundant life Jesus came to give (John 10:10). Back then all was in harmony because of love. Adam and Eve weren't supposed to lose it to the devil and with it their dominion over all things. From the beginning it had always been God's plan that Adam and Eve and their descendants cover the whole earth with people walking in communion with God, knowing nothing more than Him and His love filling everything and everyone.

It was their destiny to be unique believer-priests forever, ministering in the presence of God, and earth was to become one glorious temple for His presence. T. Desmond Alexander tells us that "this was God's blueprint for the created world."[8] This goal has not changed, and this should be the blueprint for our eschatology. God will yet accomplish the fullness of this in the end when He becomes all in all once again (Eph. 1:3–14; 1 Cor. 15:20–28) on a renewed planet Earth, which is our eternal inheritance after the resurrection (2 Pet. 3:13; Rev. 21:1). In this sense Eden ever remains the most significant piece of real estate in history.

God is eternal. He is without beginning or ending, and everything that was made was made by Him. Because we know that God is love (1 John 4:8,16), we can also safely assume that everything He has ever done comes from love. From where else could it come? These questions then arise: What is the origin of everything that isn't love? Who is to blame for its existence and the ensuing pain and sorrow that His creation has had to endure since the fall? How could God be blamed for something that couldn't have come from Him?

The Conflict Between Good and Evil Does Not Represent the Love of God

In answering these questions, let us take a step back away from the conflict in Eden and ask, "Is it important to know good and evil?" Yes, because they are both to be found at work in this present evil age (Gal. 1:4). However, knowing that God's love is greater, without conflict, and was there

[8] Taken from *From Eden to the New Jerusalem*, Copyright © 2008 by T. Desmond Alexander, p. 78. Published by Kregel Publications, Grand Rapids, MI. Used by permission of the publisher. All rights reserved.

before the fall in the Garden of Eden and will fill everything in the end after the resurrection, is paramount. The conflict between good and evil will pass, but love will never fail. Love should always prevail in our assessing of good and evil.

There are those who mistakenly suggest that because God made everything, therefore evil and its contrast, the concept of good, must also have been made by Him. However, there is no evidence in Scripture to support this, and for such a conclusion to be true, God would have to be inconsistent with His character, which is love. This goes against everything we know about God. "If his nature is perfect goodness," declared Jürgen Moltmann, "then he cannot create evil."[9] Anyway, all of His ways are done in truth (Psa. 33:4; 111:2–8); furthermore, He is not the author of confusion, satan is (1 Cor. 14:33; Jas. 3:15,16). God is the Father of lights (Jas. 1:17), and He ever remains consistent with who and what He is—love. "Since God is Love," wrote Torrance, "his love can no more cease to be love than God can cease to be God."[10]

From where then did the unlove come that swamped the Garden of Eden after they ate the forbidden fruit and cursed everything that was made?

We know for certain God has always been, and always will be, love, and there is no changing Him (Mal. 3:6). He is loving in all of His ways because He is love; it eternally proceeds from who He is, "love-in-eternal-action," as Peter Kreeft expresses it.[11] Everything God does comes from love and bears its image. Anything less than love does not come from God. As stated by Torrance, "It is then to this dynamic fullness of the Love of God which he is in himself before the very foundation of the world that all the ways and works of God in creation and redemption go back."[12]

The terms *good* and *evil* are latecomers. They do not find their origin in God but rather describe the contrast brought about by satan's choosing to rise up above the God of love "with the deliberate intention of overturning his careful ordering of creation," as Alexander wrote.[13] In this act of rebellion driven by his pride and dreams of self-exaltation, we see where the contrast to love was born. It did not come from God, nor was it in Him, nor could it be in Him. However, it was through satan's freedom to choose, which is from the gift of love, that he determined to rise higher than his calling to direct worship to God, and be above Him and receive the worship for himself. In this folly, the contrast between love and unlove was born.

> "How you are fallen from heaven, O Lucifer, son of the morning! How you are cut down to the ground, you who weakened the nations!

[13] Taken from *From Eden to the New Jerusalem*, Copyright © 2008 by T. Desmond Alexander, p. 78. Published by Kregel Publications, Grand Rapids, MI. Used by permission of the publisher. All rights reserved.

> For you have said in your heart: 'I will ascend into heaven, I will exalt my throne above the stars of God; I will also sit on the mount of the congregation on the farthest sides of the north;
> I will ascend above the heights of the clouds, I will be like the Most High.'
> Yet you shall be brought down to Sheol, to the lowest depths of the Pit."
>
> *Isa. 14:12–15*

Up until this point there was no need to say that God is good, because there was no evil to contrast with it. Evil was born of bitter envy and self-seeking (Jas. 3:14–16). God is love and cannot be selfish; otherwise, love is no longer love (1 Cor. 13), and this says it all. It is enough to fall on your knees and worship God—the Father, Son, and Holy Spirit—Who is love and everything love emanates, which is always giving. God's love doesn't know how to be anything else, and in the beginning neither did ours.

However, with satan's rebellious abuse of love the contrast plainly comes into view, and terminology is used to describe what had no precedent—*good* and *evil*. God is not good in that He is *better than*. He has no competition. He is known in the Scriptures as good *in contrast to*. Therefore, it is self-evident that God is good in contrast to satan and his evil handiwork of unlove, and the terms were not necessary until satan's rebellion against love. Bray adds, "Satan's rebellion against God was a revolt against his own condition; his hatred of the Creator was a hatred of the creation, and of himself above all."[14]

The Role of the Tree of the Knowledge of Good and Evil

Allowing the presence of the tree of the knowledge of good and evil in the Garden of Eden was an act of lovingkindness and mercy on God's part inasmuch as it enabled Him to contain man's fall, which He had foreseen and provided for (1 Pet. 1:20; Rev. 13:8). That tree preempted satan's plan to force them into his rebellion. God's foreknowledge saved the day. His love won.

Satan spoke of the tree as though it were a graduate school of higher learning that would improve man, but this was a lie that came from the father of lies (John 8:44). His intention was "to extinguish the flow of God's love to, in, and through the humans God had created," wrote Boyd.[15] Satan's counsel was a dirty trick to try to trap man, which serves as the saddest reminder that there was a day when something other than love burst onto the scene in the Garden of Eden and God had to do something about it.

The legacy of satan produced the necessity in the garden for the tree of the knowledge of good and evil and, as we have seen, judgment, for which man was totally unsuited and unequipped. Fear divides, but God's love always unites.

The legacy of God is the tree of life where those who are born at the foot of the cross are invited to eat freely and live forevermore. This is the hope of God's new creation. What a picture of true love.

And what did He do?

Before the fall of man, Eden was a perfect place. How could it have been anything less? It was where God and man communed. It was there He visited with man. It was a sanctuary. In fact, G. K. Beale informs us, "the Garden of Eden was the first archetypal temple in which the first man worshipped God."[16] Let us not forget for a moment that God is perfect love (1 John 4:8,16), and everything He does emanates from that perfection. But for that dreadful tree of the knowledge of good and evil in its midst that they weren't allowed to eat from, everything would have continued on unchanged (Gen. 2:15–17). Nevertheless, as we have already seen, it was necessary for it to be there to hasten the plans and purposes of God.

We read in the Scriptures that God "planted a garden eastward in Eden" for man to live in (Gen. 2:8). Every tree there was beautiful and good for food. One of the trees in the middle of the garden was the tree of life. It was a miraculous tree that is represented in several ways in the Holy Scriptures. It is most famous for being the tree that gave eternal life to those who ate its fruit. What a picture of Jesus Christ!

There was another tree nearby that was known as the tree of the knowledge of good and evil. It wasn't a tree that gave hope and life. Instead, it came with a warning—they were informed by God not to eat of it without devastating results, even death. Psychologist Paul Tournier described the situation this way: "God knows to what calamities, even to death itself, Adam will expose himself if he eats of that tree, if he aspires to be his own God, judging for himself what is good and evil. It is not out of caprice, but in order to protect him against these consequences that God forbids him to eat of the tree. When he does eat, he brings upon himself...the calamities which flow from his act...."[17]

It was planted with the foreknowledge of God that sooner or later the tempter would seduce man into eating of its fruit. One thing we can know for sure is that God didn't put it there to tempt man (Jas. 1:13), but He allowed man to be exposed to it and the possibility of eating its fruit.

To be God's lovers forever, man had to triumph over satan's rebellion. Love sets us free to choose for ourselves; it is not a jailer. Furthermore, because love covers, it provides a remedy for sin before mistakes are even made, rather than looking for an opportunity to expose them after they are made. Satan was the tempter, and God had catered for his evil schemes. This is what love always does. Love covers; judgmentalism exposes (Prov. 10:12; 16:27; 17:9; Jas. 2:13; 1 Pet. 4:8). Amazingly, grace is what we call this incredible display of undeserved love.

Out of the overflow of God's great love He made man in His image to live by the fullness of the love shared between the Father, Son, and Holy Spirit. That there is no room in that love for the conflict created by the knowledge of good and evil, and the judgmentalism that it produces, is self-evident. If the eating of the fruit was necessary in order to know God or experience Him, then I would like to know, why did eating it bring death and not life; give satan, and not God, the advantage over man; and have a devastating effect on man's fellowship with God, making him more attuned to fellowship with satan? All of those things are contrary to God's plan for man to be His eternal lover.

The temptation to eat of the tree of the knowledge of good and evil seems to have been inevitable, something that man would have to get over on his journey to becoming one with God forevermore. Truly love is patient and kind. Yes, God had a backup plan from the beginning, and it was big. It would include not only the restoration of man but also of all creation. In other words, "The redemption of the cosmos will come with the redemption of humanity," notes Sandra L. Richter.[18] Furthermore, His plan of redemption, "a recovering and restoring of the original," as Meredith G. Kline stated,[19] would also involve the downfall of satan and everything he had influenced. This is the big picture. Good and evil will not continue on into eternity after the final judgment. Only love will prevail.

Getting Adam and Eve to eat from the tree of the knowledge of good and evil was important for satan. From his darkened point of view and his limited knowledge, he saw it as an opportunity to try to rise up over God and be worshiped like Him by man. How so? By usurping the authority of man and his dominion over the earth, taking control of God's creation, rearranging everything to suit his dark purposes, and making himself the god of this world. Thus he intended to rob God of His lover—man.

This is why the Scriptures speak of the devil as the "ruler of this world" (John 12:31; 14:30; 16:11) and also the "god of this age" (2 Cor. 4:4). He was dreaming big, but God is the Alpha and Omega, and He knew everything from the start to the finish. As far as He was concerned, the Redeemer had already been slain from the foundation of the world (Rev. 13:8) and His plan of salvation put in force. In the words of C. S. Lewis, "God saw the crucifixion in the act of creating the first nebula."[20] Thus, satan's attempt was a lost cause from the start. Man's fall, on the other hand, was a guaranteed win because of that plan of salvation. It would only be a matter of time before God would send His Son to earth where love would triumph over fear and redeemed man would be His forevermore.

Thus everything will have come full circle, and man will have returned to Eden. "What began in the Garden of Eden finds its completion at the end of history," Grenz points out.[21] "The result of all this will be Paradise Regained," wrote Murray J. Harris, "a return to the pristine state of the entire material order where God was 'all in all', universally supreme."[22]

Yes, God was aware of good and evil, but His love was not the source of it; satan's bitter envy and self-seeking prior to Eden were. He was the one who rose up against love and failed. It is he who is the father of lies, the accuser of the brethren, the deceiver, the tempter, and the destroyer who, having fallen from love, manufactured his own realm of darkness in contrast to the light of God's love, dishonestly calling it light (2 Cor. 11:14). Fear is his domain, and love is God's domain; the knowledge of good and evil, which is the source of all accusation, criticism, and judgment, has no place in love but only in fear and torment, which are haunted by the uncertain. You can blame satan for all this.

Living by God's love in His Kingdom is man's highest calling. It raises him above the fray. It is the lens through which God's people view life. This doesn't mean they are supposed to be over-emotional, blindly tolerant pushovers that live unrestrained lives full of misconduct, calling it love. God's love is much bigger than that. There is a world of difference between rising to a new ethic that is love-motivated from heaven, and the kind of earthly love that ruins people's lives and runs satan's kingdom of darkness.

God's love is unique and is found in Him alone. It is always giving (*agapē*). It is full of surprises that reveal the character of God, not the character of fallen man. This is why believers don't need to live by the tree of the knowledge of good and evil to know God, in spite of the fact that it is everywhere, even in their flesh. However, since they were saved, God's love is now in them through the Holy Spirit, and they have a new capacity to live by God's love, which is higher. For them, life is as it was in Eden—all about being in fellowship with God, Who is love, and bringing this experience into everything they do. As John put it, "As He is, so are we in this world" (1 John 4:17).

It is to this that every preacher should make his appeal when ministering to God's people (Gal. 4:19). This was the truth behind the Sermon on the Mount; it laid out the difference between living by love from a heart that was in communion with God, and the religious world's unlove. Living by God's love is greater than anything that tree could ever produce. God is love, and everything He is and does comes from that love. When we walk with God empowered by His love, that tree becomes a non-issue.

Today we live in a critical world where knowledge abounds and the revelation of God and His love has been overlooked. We have become a society of barkers and biters, and woe betide those who don't come into agreement with us; after all, our understanding of right and wrong is superior. And so we judge one another and pride ourselves in knowing better and knowing more. Everyone seems to be crusading for something or other, and they know they have the answers. The presumption thus born in our personal judgment of things has sown the seeds of division and anarchy everywhere in society, our churches, and our homes. Pride and knowledge have become man's savior. Instead of love taking over, it is in retreat. Furthermore, we have incorrectly sealed God in a box and labeled it "right and wrong" and chased after unlove, hoping to find Him there. What a sad mistake.

Our mandate is not to become specialists in good and evil, because this will only exacerbate the conflict that has been going on in man since the fall in the garden. Our rest is in Christ, our standing is in His righteousness by grace, and our mandate is to live by His Calvary love through the Spirit. We are a people of faith, and not judgment. The Scriptures tell us, "Do not be overcome by evil, but overcome evil with good" (Rom. 12:21). How do we do this? By being motivated by love rather than the conflict that arises out of judging between good and evil and trying to match up and never being certain that we have. This is how we bring our fellowship with God into everything—living by the grace of the Lord Jesus, the love of the Father, and the communion of the Holy Spirit (2 Cor. 13:14).

The Knowledge of Good and Evil, and Love

We know this for sure: Adam and Eve's gaining the knowledge of good and evil didn't deliver what satan promised. In fact, it took them away from love and became the foundation for satan's cosmic system of fear. "They passed from the realm of innocence into the realm of judgment," writes Boyd, "where the knowledge of good and evil rather than love of God reigns supreme."[23] All it produced was judgmentalism and dissatisfaction on a monumental scale that man was completely unqualified to deal with, and along with it, death. In fact, as surely as Christ's cosmos is love-based, satan's cosmos is fear-based, brought about by the conflict of knowing good and evil without the love to conquer either (1 John 2:15,16; 4:18; Rom. 8:15).

It is sad to recognize that many Christians are still fighting the same battle as Adam and Eve, even though Christ has remedied the problem: Should we or should we not trust in God's love and live by it, or should we keep on trying to better ourselves and live by the law-grace mixture that prevails in most evangelical circles? Christians who know Jesus and His grace and truth are those who have fought this internal battle and surrendered to love as the only answer.

Is there such a thing as knowing good and evil? Of course there is. Adam and Eve found this out firsthand after they ate of the fruit of that tree. And they wished they never had! As Bray put it, they "could not apologize for their mistake and put the fruit back on the tree....What was done was done, and there could be no going back to their earlier state."[24] It didn't help their relationship to God. It brought it to ruin.

Today there is good and there is evil in this world, and this is satan's world. Unfortunately, to live in it we all need to be ever aware of both. Nevertheless, as God's children we live by love, standing in Christ's righteousness by grace alone, knowing that it is by faith in these that we reign in life. Surely in God's kingdom, love must triumph over the knowledge of good and evil, making Christ's churches safe zones for His new creation people. The conflict of good and evil has ruined this world and made it an ugly, critical, dark place full of fear and hiding. It has devastated us at our core, and our need for loving, trusting relationships. Judging leaves us limping through life, full of unforgiveness and fear, trusting no one, and this is exactly what satan wants. It shrinks us, leaving us insecure and full of bitterness. It violates us and makes us vulnerable to confusion.

God is love. Everything God does comes from His love. In the end, all judgment is His because only His love is qualified to recognize the difference between love and "unlove," which for us humans is clouded by fear. Love is full of light. Love is full of life. Love made man, and because of it man needs love. As Allan Coppedge put it, "God desires that we know his fullness. That fullness is love."[25]

And this brings us to the subject of whether love and the knowledge of good and evil are compatible. They are not, and my thesis is that inevitably one must reign over the other. Jesus settled the issue when He said, "I am the way, the truth and the life" (John 14:6). This revelation clarified the superior role of grace and truth—it is the Son of God, and not the knowledge of good and evil. He alone must reign. His will must prevail. His words must be embraced. Walking in His footsteps renders us free indeed. This implies that love, embodied in Jesus, is the way, the truth, and the life for His new humanity. We don't live by carnal information; we live by the revelation of the Son of God. This is also how we grow from glory to glory (2 Cor. 3:18).

Five Contrasts Between the Lifestyles of Love and Unlove
(Romans 5)

Lifestyle of Love *Feeding on the love of God in Christ's righteousness, standing in grace*	**Lifestyle of Unlove** *Feeding on the tree of the knowledge of good and evil*
No Condemnation	Judgment (Gen. 3:7a)
Love	Fear
Grace	Works
Freedom	Bondage
A Life-Giver	A Killer

We are a word of faith people (Rom. 10:8). Everything we need to know about truthful living has its roots in Him—love. When you live by His example, you don't need to be impressed by anything else, because what you are living is how the Son of God lived, and this is enough for His Father, "whose only authority is compassion," Nouwen stated.[26] We must read the Holy Scriptures through the eyes of God's love, or we won't interpret it properly. Love wrote it. Reading it should put fear to flight and establish love as our best motive.

Jesus has overcome satan's world system—we believers are crucified to the world, and it has been crucified to us (Gal. 6:14). We live in another cosmic dimension, the kingdom of love. It is vain to try to marry the two.

God's Love Is the Answer to the Conflict Created by Good and Evil

Read these scriptures, and see the important role love plays in that holy book. "This is My commandment, that you love one another as I have loved you. Greater love has no one than this, than to lay down one's life for his friends" (John 15:12,13). "Owe no one anything except to love one another, for he who loves another has fulfilled the law" (Rom. 13:8). "Just as He chose us in Him before the foundation of the world, that we should be holy and without blame before Him in love" (Eph. 1:4). "That Christ may dwell in your hearts through faith; that you, being rooted and grounded in love" (Eph. 3:17). "And walk in love, as Christ also has loved us and given Himself for us, an offering and a sacrifice to God for a sweet-smelling aroma" (Eph. 5:2). "That their hearts may be encouraged, being knit together in love, and attaining to all riches of the full assurance of understanding, to the knowledge of the mystery of God, both of the Father and of Christ" (Col. 2:2). "Remembering without ceasing your work of faith, labor of love, and patience of hope in our Lord Jesus Christ in the sight of our God and Father" (1 Thess. 1:3). "Hold fast the pattern of sound words which you have heard from me, in faith and love which are in Christ Jesus" (2 Tim. 1:13). "And we have known and believed the love that God has for us. God is love, and he who abides in love abides in God, and God in him" (1 John 4:16). "Though I speak with the tongues of men and of angels, but have not love, I have become sounding brass or a clanging cymbal. And though I have the gift of prophecy, and understand all mysteries and all knowledge, and though I have all faith, so that I could remove mountains, but have not love, I am nothing. And though I bestow all my goods to feed the poor, and though I give my body to be burned, but have not love, it profits me nothing" (1 Cor. 13:1–3).

The knowledge of good and evil is not a virtue. It is a vice. It creates tension. It is a bondage that strangles love and often manipulates the truth, leaving its victims unsure of themselves and afraid. It is an invitation to see what it is like to live without God and be in tune with the devilish world of unlove. It has set man at odds with one another ever since. Love, God's love through Christ by the Holy Spirit, is the answer, and the knowledge of good and evil is not. In fact, it is vain for man to think that he could be like

God in all things and always know what is good, what is evil, and how to judge between the two (Jas. 4:12), even though he owns a Bible. Judgment is God's domain, and we are told to "judge nothing before the time" (1 Cor. 4:5). Our righteous understanding of life comes from Christ alone, not from that awful tree. Love sets us free.

When God placed man in the Garden of Eden, He knew the risk He was taking, and He was willing to do so because love demands freedom and could do no less. Coppedge states, "If one of the purposes of creation is to have persons share in the fellowship of love, then freedom is an absolute necessity."[27] In fact, as Peter Kreeft explains, "The connection between the fall and love is freedom. Love…frees the beloved.…Without that freedom to sin there is also no freedom to love."[28] And Lewis informs us, "He caused things to be other than Himself that, being distinct, they might learn to love Him, and achieve union instead of mere sameness. Thus He also cast His bread upon the waters."[29]

The Side Effects of Knowing Good and Evil (*Genesis 3:7-13*)

7 Then the eyes of both of them were **opened**[1], and
they **knew**[2] that they were naked; and they sewed fig
leaves together and **made**[3] themselves coverings.
8 And they heard the sound of the Lord God walking
in the garden in the cool of the day, and Adam and his

wife **hid**[4] themselves from the presence of the Lord God
among the trees of the garden.
9 Then the Lord God called to Adam and said to him,
"Where are you?"
10 So he said, "I heard Your voice in the garden, and I
was **afraid**[5] because I was naked; and I hid myself."
11 And He said, "Who told you that you were naked?
Have you eaten from the tree of which I commanded
you that you should not eat?"
12 Then the man said, "**The woman**[6] whom You gave to
be with me, she gave me of the tree, and I ate."
13 And the Lord God said to the woman, "What is this
you have done?" The woman said, "The serpent deceived
me, and I ate."

The Hebrew meaning of the above words in **bold**:

1. "opened"—Heb. *paqach*, to open (the senses, esp. the eyes) = ***aware***

2. "knew"—Heb. *yada*, to know by seeing = ***guilty***

3. "made"—Heb. *asah*, to do or make = ***works***

4. "hid"—Heb. *chaba*, to do secretly = ***hid***

5. "afraid"—Heb. *yare*, to fear, cause to frighten = ***afraid***

6. "The woman and the man" set up a lifestyle of ***blaming***, ***excuses***, and ***victim mentality*** that mankind has been using ever since.

The knowledge of good and evil was never intended for the benefit of God's creation.

The telling of the story of the fall of mankind goes like this: There weren't only three—God, Adam, and Eve—in that fair garden; there was a fourth—satan—who had every intention of spoiling it all and ruining the loving fellowship between man and his God. Satan could not bear what God had done for His creation (Psa. 8), neither did he want them to have what he had lost. To achieve this, he chose to appeal to one of man's best qualities—the ability to reason—and deceive him into disobeying God's command not to eat of the forbidden fruit, thereby ceding control to him. Because they had no experience in dishonesty, they failed this test (Gen. 3:1–7). Their curiosity without restraint won, or in the words of Gerald Bray, "temptation got the better of their curiosity and they fell."[30] From that day on good and evil have been in every man. It is a problem that we all live with, and it's not going away until the end.

Isn't it a shame that in God's kingdom of love we have to contend with satan's world of good and evil? Communion with God was lost that day, and man was left hopelessly alone in a world that had become his enemy. It is only in love that the truth of God is born, and His world will become a better place for all to live in.

The decision to go against God's command was a violation of the perfect love that existed between them and

Him, and even a "rejection of the God in whose love we are created and by whose love we are sustained," stated Nouwen;[31] therefore, nothing would ever be the same again. Bray adds, "The sin of Adam and Eve was fundamentally a rejection of God's love for them."[32] After eating the forbidden fruit, all they knew was that something frightening had happened to them and their world, and they hid from love (Gen. 3:8–12). The knowledge they gained from the tree of good and evil wasn't the blessing they thought it would be. "The cost to them far outweighed any benefit they may have received, and from that perspective their sin made no sense at all," Bray tells us.[33] In fact, it placed a burden on them that they could not bear—a curse. "Adam involved the whole creation in his disobedience," wrote Oscar Cullmann, "and now the creation is subject, with Adam, to perishability."[34]

Satan the great manipulator was the only winner that day. He knew all along what he was doing, and it suited his dark plans perfectly to get them to make the same mistake he did—look away from God and humility to self and pride for their future. Having done so, mankind and his home, planet Earth, came under the sway of the evil one, and there was nothing they could do about it. All was lost.

By taking his advice, they had surrendered to a new lord (John 14:30; 8:44) who had every intention of controlling everything and everyone to suit his dark purposes. In their act of rebellion, as Alexander put it, "harmony gives way to chaos."[35] The perfect gave way to the imperfect, and everything created groaned and travailed to return to Eden (Rom. 8:22–25).

We often hear people demand, "Where was God?" in this calamity, or that heartbreaking experience, or some personal loss. Others in their frustration have even coined the phrase "an act of God" to describe terrible things that happen, such as floods, lightning strikes, volcanic eruptions, sickness, or even death. What they don't seem to realize, however, is that God gave the dominion of this world to man, and that by taking satan's advice and eating the forbidden fruit, he lost that dominion to satan and his dark hoards who know nothing about love and everything about lying, deceiving, and destroying, always "seeking to separate us from the love of God" and "ruling over the lives of those who live far from the love of God," as John Howard Yoder described.[36] Perhaps next time there is a tragic plane crash or a horrible natural disaster, we should call it what it is—an act of satan that breaks the heart of our loving God. This problem will not change until satan is cast into the lake of fire forever and the old heavens and earth are made new. In the meantime believers have been given the authority to take dominion over all things and reign in life by grace through Christ's victory over satan on their behalf. Life is not always fair, but God always remains love.

[35] Taken from *From Eden to the New Jerusalem* Copyright © 2008 by T. Desmond Alexander, p. 79. Published by Kregel Publications, Grand Rapids, MI. Used by permission of the publisher. All rights reserved.

A Plan from the Beginning

It was always God's plan that a new creation, a second creation if you please, would be born of the Spirit (John 3:3–8) out of the old. This is what the Old Testament prophets promised (1 Pet. 1:10–12). This new birth, or spiritual rebirth, was not man's idea but God's. He knew the first creation would hopelessly fall, and so He planned for a second creation to rise up out of the ashes of their defeat by the power of the Spirit—brothers and sisters of Jesus, His only begotten Son (Mark 3:34,35; Heb. 2:11,12, 17). Love made a way. No wonder the Scriptures say that Jesus is the way, the truth, and the life (John 14:6).

It is God's intention that a new creation made alive by the Holy Spirit will return to Eden-like conditions in the new heavens and the new earth in the end, and it is to this family that all believers from both testaments belong. We are destined to walk with God forever. As Richter states, "We are headed back to Eden, with all of heaven urging us on!"[37] And she adds, "It is with the New Jerusalem that Eden is restored and the people of God return to the place of God with full access to the presence of God."[38] Anthony A. Hoekema wrote, "At the end of history we see the new heavens and the new earth, which will far surpass in splendor all that we have seen before."[39]

The Scriptures teach that the resurrected Christ is the firstfruits of this promised new creation that will return to

Eden in the end, of which God says, "Behold, I make all things new" (Rev. 21:5).

CHAPTER 2

The Day After Their Disobedience:

A Legacy of Criticism

In the garden, love was all that Adam and Eve knew. Their relationship to God was everything. Truly they were naive to anything else, in the best sense of the word. They were as pure as the love that birthed them. The knowledge of good and evil was completely foreign to them. "As innocent creatures," writes Grenz, "Adam and Eve had not yet been confronted with the awful distinction between good and evil."[1] They had no knowledge of what good and evil were, nor did they see any need for it, "nor would Adam and Eve or their descendants have analyzed their experience in terms of good or evil," notes Boyd.[2] Love was enough, and it was in them and everywhere around them. God and man walked together in harmony. It was a safe place without fear. "This was Adam and Eve's perfect world," wrote Sandra L. Richter, "...the *people* of God in the *place* of God dwelling in the *presence* of God."[3]

There was no discord. For that matter, what was discord? They didn't know. It didn't exist. Theirs was a world made by love, and there was no need for anything else. This love shielded them from satan's rebellious cosmos of unlove and the conflicting knowledge of good and evil that was waiting in the shadows to ruin their fellowship with God.

I have become persuaded over the years that a better understanding of the negative effects of that tragic day and how it ruined their relationship to God, and what He has done to remedy it through His Son Jesus Christ on the cross, will not only help to clarify the Christian message according to the Scriptures, but make it very relevant to us all today. This is especially true in light of the many paradoxes of life that have no explanation outside of a spiritual conflict taking place on earth between good and evil behind the scenes.

There were at least eight negative consequences set in motion that terrible day, and how God put right the wrongs brought about by their tragic eating of the fruit of the tree of the knowledge of good and evil is what I deal with throughout this book. Christ, as the second Adam (1 Cor. 15:45,47), "defeated the deception of the devil and reopened access to the tree of life," stated Paul Minear,[4] by not falling prey to satan's temptations, but living a perfect life of love, thus qualifying Himself to die on the cross and rise again triumphantly on the third day over satan, his kingdom of darkness, and all sin. What the first Adam lost in the Garden of Eden, the second Adam, Jesus Christ, purchased back on the cross so that salvation could be offered freely by His grace to as many as believed. "In Christ the dominion of Adam is once more restored," wrote L. S. Thornton.[5]

Adam and Eve's eating of the forbidden fruit (1) interrupted the purity of love between God and humanity; (2) separated humanity from being able to commune with God; (3) darkened humanity's minds because of the absence of God's love and the truth that emanates from it; (4) created animosity between humanity, God, and one another; (5) aligned humanity as a race with satan's rebellion; (6) opened the door to satan and his cosmos to have dominion over humanity and their planet; (7) brought satan's judgment on humanity and their planet; and (8) enabled satan to rob man of his superabundant life and fill him with fear unto death. Let us briefly consider these devastating results.

The Fall Interrupted the Purity of Love Between God and Humanity

In the beginning the Garden of Eden was full of God—that is to say, not only was He there, but everything there was made by Him and was good in His sight. Because we know God is love, it must have been full of the purity of that love. There was room for nothing else, as Boyd tells us, "but the unsurpassable fullness and joy of living in fellowship with a God who is unsurpassable love and joy."[6]

It was a most perfect environment. God was comfortable there, and man was comfortable there. Adam and Eve were aware of nothing but love, and this was as God wanted it to remain. In his description of the first Adam, C. S. Lewis wrote, "God came first in his love and in his thought, and that without painful effort. In perfect cyclic movement, being, power and joy descended from God to man in the form of gift and returned from man to God in the form of obedient love and ecstatic adoration."[7]

Today we can't relate to a world that is only full of love the way it was in Eden before the fall. Since the eating of the fruit, love has been corrupted, and life has become hard without it; everyone lives with the threat of death hanging over them (Rom. 5:12; Heb. 2:14,15). This is even true today among believers, who are a part of God's new creation. Even though they have the love of God implanted in them (Rom. 5:5) and its parameters defined for them (1 Cor. 13:4–7), and the Holy Spirit has empowered them to walk in it (Eph. 5:2), it still takes sacrifice and a whole lot of faith to do so. God's love is foreign to our flesh, and this means that God, Who is love, has also become a foreigner to humanity.

Because they had no exposure to anything but love, and because we know from 1 Corinthians 13 and other scriptures what love looks like, there was no way that Adam and Eve could have had the remotest idea that the eating of the forbidden fruit would affect their world of love.

Nevertheless, it did. It interrupted the purity of love between God and humanity and "introduced enmity into a creation that had only known harmony," noted Grenz.[8] The shock must have been devastating to them. What was released that day by gaining the knowledge of good and evil contaminated everything, including their life-source, love. They were caught off guard by this and became afraid. They felt alienated from their best friend, God. Being afraid and hiding was also something new for them, which "indicated that the pristine fellowship with the Creator had been broken," Grenz points out.[9] For the first time they were "fearful of being caught in flagrant disobedience," wrote Minear. "Their nakedness symbolized their helplessness; they had no excuse that would stand up in God's eyes."[10] They had never felt this way before, and they didn't know until then that they could. Satan's counsel turned out to be a lie, and they were not better off for having embraced it; in fact, they had traded in love for the conflicting knowledge of good and evil and only gained fear, judgmentalism, loneliness, and an entrance into satan's cosmos of darkness filled with love's impostors. This opened the door to other things taking the place of what man was created for—loving fellowship with God.

Thus the pure love in which they lived was polluted. Knowing good and evil had done its dirty work, and I believe that this revelation is still doing the same today. Who would ever have thought, from a religious point of view, that knowing good and evil kicks out pure love? Surely it should have had the opposite effect, but it never does. In fact, that tree planted in the midst of God's garden filled with His love came with a warning label: "Stay away from me because my fruit is a killer! It will turn you into an unqualified judge of things." Here is how Tournier described the result of Adam and Eve's supposed gain: "There is no neutral position between good and evil; we must pass judgment, pronounce a verdict, say who is guilty and who is not, under pain of denying our faith, our morality and our humanity.... But there is no one who does not suffer...from being in conflict with others and from being an agent of division rather than of harmony among men, even though he is quite certain of being in the right."[11]

God's pure love transcends the knowledge of good and evil and the critical world this creates. The conflict does not come from God, and not realizing this has troubled many. Only love comes from God, nothing more and nothing less. It is in this alone that He is Who He is, the one, true, holy God. Amazingly, the purity of God's love is what separates Him and puts Him in a class all by Himself. He is the holy God who dwells in light inaccessible (1 Tim. 6:15,16), and it is a light that emanates from Who He is—Love.

This leaves no place for the conflict of good and evil.

No one needs the knowledge of good or evil in a world of love, because love is harmless and life-giving (Rom. 13:10). In this world's environment of unlove, living by God's love is naive in the most holy way.

Of course, some might say that if God is neither good nor evil, but rather love, why then did Jesus say that no one but God is good (Luke 18:19)? In answer, we should keep in mind that Jesus was using a term of comparison that religious man could relate to, and He was describing the chasm that exists between God and man. Love is who God is, and good and evil are the behavior of man estranged from the purity of that love. Good and evil are descriptive terms of contrast and conflict. Religion not founded on love always misses the point. For example, Jerome (AD 347–420), a father of the Latin church, said, "Good, better, best. Never let it rest. 'Til your good is better and your better is best." There is not a quicker way to wear yourself out in the flesh or set yourself up to judge those around you than to take this advice.

The Fall Separated Humanity from Being Able to Commune with God

Eating from the tree of the knowledge of good and evil separated humanity from being able to commune with God. How so? They lost their common ground, love. Adam and

Eve were no longer capable of living by the love that once filled who they were and everything they did. It had become tainted by the tree and cursed. Because "God changes not" (Mal. 3:6), and man changed, they lost their common ground and could no longer commune with one another.

When man ate of the forbidden fruit, he chose his way out of God's world of love into the crippling world of the knowledge of good and evil and everything that came from that exposure, even death. As a result, Adam and Eve forfeited the opportunity of eating from the tree of life, and death now reigned in its place over them and their world. Therefore, it isn't hard to realize that their world was no longer a place where God could dwell. As Richter described it, "Intimacy with God, which was the essence of humanity's existence, [was] shattered."[12] Thus communion with God was lost forever because man could no longer speak God's language of love, but instead spoke a language learned from the knowledge of good and evil. "Adam, as one who knows *tob* [good] and *ra* [evil] and has fallen from unity into dividedness, can no longer stand before the Creator," wrote Dietrich Bonhoeffer.[13]

One of the most interesting things about the knowledge of good and evil and its incompatibility with love is how it left man unable to live in either world, Eden or the one they had chosen instead by default. Many don't seem to realize that no matter how much good we know or evil we avoid, we can never attain to either or qualify ourselves to have communion with God. Only God is good. To know God is beyond us because His love ever remains out of our reach. As we have already seen, it is only by grace through faith in the work of the cross that we can once again experience the love of God and return to communion with Him. Trying to do so by our own works is hopeless.

The knowledge of good and evil separated humanity from being able to commune with God because:

1. Love is Who God is, and He can be no less.

2. The natural man is full of the knowledge of good and evil, and he can be no more.

3. Light and darkness cannot fellowship any more than love and the knowledge of good and evil can abide together.

4. To fellowship with God is impossible for the natural man and will remain so, unless he is reborn of the Spirit and God's love is shed abroad in his heart miraculously.

5. For God to ever abide with men, they must choose to walk in God's love by faith, empowered by the Spirit of grace within, and only Christians who are full of the Holy Spirit can do this (John 14:22,23; 15:9; 1 John 4:12–16).

6. God cannot fellowship with anything less than His own love.

The Fall Darkened Humanity's Minds Because of the Absence of God's Love and the Truth That Emanates from It

God is love, and all truth emanates from the light of that love. This is why Jesus, Who was the express image of His Father, is known as the light of the world (John 1:4–10; 8:12; 12:46).

Love is light. Fear is darkness.

In the absence of God's love, fear has prevailed, and as the Scriptures put it, "the [world] lies in darkness until now" (1 John 5:19; 2:8,9; John 3:19).

There are some very interesting phrases that Paul uses in his Ephesian epistle, referring to unbelievers. He reminds us that their understanding is darkened, alienated from the life of God, ignorant, hardhearted, past feeling, and given over to sin (Eph. 4:17–19). He then said something most interesting: "You have not so learned Christ" (vv. 20–24). He concluded with this: "Be kind to one another, tender-hearted, forgiving one another, just as God in Christ also forgave you,…and walk in love, as Christ also has loved us" (Eph. 4:32–5:2).

Being helplessly trapped in the conflicting knowledge of good and evil, as opposed to being full of God's love, humanity's mind is darkened and cannot, without miraculous intervention, know truth, as it only emanates from the light of God's love. This will be clarified in a later chapter. However, truth that is not put into the context of God's love is dangerous and misrepresents what He wants to get across. Man is completely unable to achieve this on his own because:

1. God is love, and the Scriptures tell us He is full of light, and in Him is no darkness at all (1 John 1:5); therefore, His love emanates light. Thus Jesus is the light of the world (John 8:12; 9:5).

2. You cannot separate God's love and the truth that emanates from it any more than you can divorce the darkness of humanity's minds from the absence of God's love in them.

3. For believers, to love as God loves is to come alive and be filled with all the light of God.

4. To not have the love of God in you is to be full of darkness, and as Jesus said, when the darkness that is in you is called light, how great is that darkness (Matt. 6:23).

5. Truth comes from the light of God's love, and not from the conflicting knowledge of good and evil.

6. God's new creation has disciplined ("sound," 2 Tim. 1:7) minds that recognize and know the truth because of the parameters of God's love in them through the power of the Spirit and the Word (Rom. 10:8,9).

The Fall Created Animosity Between Humanity, God, and One Another

Man's eating from the forbidden tree produced an unforeseen animosity full of fear between them and God, with one another, and what is most interesting, within themselves. When love prevailed prior to what theologians like to call "the fall of man," purity, peace, gentleness, submission, mercy, and good fruits, etc., prevailed within and without—so says James the brother of Jesus (Jas. 3:17,18).

All humanity are known as sinners who have fallen short of the glory of God, because sin falls short of God's love (Rom. 3:23). This misunderstood word (sin) describes everything that isn't full of the love of God. This is the condemnation that only the cross, which is the apex of God's love, can remove from man's guilty conscience. To come to Christ is to turn from sin's unlove to God's perfect love and be saved. The Law Covenant's Ten Commandments were a stark reminder to the Jews of how far from love they had fallen. The Grace Covenant has set believers free to rise up once again and live by the glory of His love the way it was in Eden before the conflicting knowledge of good and evil sank us so low. Fellowship lost has at last been regained.

It is man's inner conflict, created by having replaced love with the knowledge of good and evil, that is the problem. Pride now controls where the humility of God's love once ruled. This is where the worst damage was done. Hence, James speaks of "wars and fights" and great conflict within, creating all kinds of negativity that proves that our friendship is with satan's cosmos and not God. Whether we like it or not, we are at war with one another and ourselves because we are at war with God, Who is love (Jas. 4:1–4). And we can't afford to forget for a moment that the knowledge of good and evil from our limited perspective is the cause of it all. As Lewis noted, "[M]an is now a horror to God and to himself and a creature ill-adapted to the universe not because God made him so but because he has made himself so by the abuse of his free will."[14] And Grenz adds, "Through this act, Adam and Eve destroyed the fellowship with God, each other, and creation that had characterized life in the Garden."[15] The knowledge of good and evil did not, and does not, benefit man.

God hopes that we will respond to His Calvary love with a heart of gratitude that turns into "much love" (Luke 7:47). In fact, He expects His love for us and in us to become the driving force behind everything we do (2 Cor.

5:14; 1 John 4:10,11). When this is so, we truly become God's lovers, and He comes to abide with us and bless us with heaven's best (John 15:9–17). At last love's light will shine in us and through us; in fact, it will fill our world and make it as beautiful as Eden.

In perhaps what is the most beautifully revealing passage in the Scriptures about God and His love for us and how jealous He is of our affection for lesser things, He says of the Holy Spirit within believers, "The Spirit who dwells in us yearns jealously" (Jas. 4:5). And what for? For us to be full of His love alone and to allow it to change everything about us. Isn't it amazing that we have come so far from this truth that it takes humility, what Lewis described as a "painful effort,"[16] to accept this?

This war within has also affected everything that is without. It has filled the world with hatred, causing endless wars between nations, and this will continue until the end when the coming Prince of Peace takes over the world by force and sets up His kingdom of love. Why is this so?

1. Because God is love, it is complete and without admixture or division.

2. It is the love between the Father, Son, and Holy Spirit that unifies Them, and without this love there can be no unity anywhere.

3. Because love is the bond of perfection, in the absence of God's love everything unravels and discord is born (Col. 3:14).

4. Only God's love creates unity by the Spirit of love.

5. The knowledge of good and evil does not unify; it divides and creates conflict.

6. Man's knowledge is relative and, therefore, limited and unreliable (1 Cor. 3:19).

The Fall Aligned Humanity as a Race with Satan's Rebellion

This is perhaps the most addressed topic regarding the fateful mistake Adam and Eve made when they listened to satan. He rebelled, and he deceived them into rebellion. From that day on he has had his way with us (John 8:44). This world (cosmos) is a system ("cosmic" arrangement) based on rebellion against God and therefore against love, and it doesn't matter to him whether it comes from the knowledge of good or evil. He is in a fight against God, and we are caught up in it with him in this arrangement.

There are no exceptions to this, and whether man is always aware of this or not, humanity walks "according to the course of this world, according to the prince of the power of the air, the spirit who now works in the sons of disobedience, among whom also we all once conducted ourselves" (Eph. 2:1–3).

Thus we have the record of humanity's alignment with satan's rebellion against God and His love:

1. Man's knowledge of good and evil came about because man rebelled against God's love the way satan did.

2. Since the fall man has been both good and evil all the time, and there are no exceptions to this; therefore, man always falls short of God's glory (love).

3. To draw from the knowledge of good and evil alone is to consciously and subconsciously rebel against God's cosmos of love, which is neither good nor evil, and align yourself with satan's cosmos.

4. To be saved from this curse, men must repent of trusting in their knowledge of good and evil for their salvation, trust in the love of God manifest in Christ, and make Him their Lord and Savior by grace through faith alone.

5. The only way for God's new creation to undo the rebellion is to stop living solely by the conflicting knowledge of good and evil, because if there was any redeeming quality to be found in this, God

would have told them to eat of this tree rather than refrain from doing so.

6. The conflicting knowledge of good and evil has done nothing but bring harm to humanity, and it has taken the attention off the love of God and put it on man and his works. It has corrupted man's senses. We are divinely destined to live by love alone.

In stark contrast to this rebellion, however, being filled with the Holy Spirit is all about speaking, singing, and giving thanks with hearts full of gratitude to God and in submission to one another (Eph. 5:8–20), which are all a manifestation of the Holy Spirit pouring out God's love in our hearts (Rom. 5:5).

The Fall Opened the Door to Satan and His Cosmos to Have Dominion over Humanity and Their Planet

God in His love made man in His image and gave him dominion over all His creation (Psa. 8). "Man as created was already crowned with glory and honor," wrote Kline, "for made in the likeness of the enthroned Glory, a little lower than the angels…, man was invested with official authority to exercise dominion as priest-king in God's earthly courts."[17] It was His desire that the earth be ruled by their offspring and spread His love everywhere even as it was in everything.

When Adam and Eve chose to believe satan rather than God and ate of the forbidden fruit, they violated the terms and conditions that God had made with them. Their bad choices gave satan dominion over them and their world, and when they were expelled from the Garden of Eden, they left God's world of love, light, and life and became subject to satan's world of fear, darkness, and death. As Thornton stated, man "by false independence lost control,"[18] was exiled "from his true home which is the paradise of God's creative design," and found himself burdened with "the endless task of endeavouring to turn chaos into cosmos."[19] And James D. G. Dunn points out, "At all events, humankind in seeking to grasp for God's glory (to be like God) had lost even the share in that glory which they had originally been given."[20] Satan succeeded in usurping control over God's good creation and made everything evil by force.

This condition remained unchallenged until the cross where Christ "disarmed principalities and powers" and "made a public spectacle of them, triumphing over them" (Col. 2:14,15), and became Lord over all on behalf of His church (Acts 2:32–35; Eph. 1:19–23). Since then satan has been exposed, his kingdom of darkness put in disarray, and his dominion over man spoiled, because Christ has given His authority to His new creation (Matt. 28:18–20; Mark

16:15–20). Satan has lost control, and we have gained it through Christ. We now rule by faith. Satan is not well on planet Earth anymore. He is a wounded, dying foe that the least of God's children can silence in Jesus' name. Thus the one who bound us is now bound by us. He has lost his control over death and, along with it, fear (Heb. 2:14,15).

How did humanity lose their dominion to satan and his cosmos?

1. Satan is the author of confusion (1 Cor. 14:33), who through his rebellion gave rise to the conflict between the knowledge of good and evil and God's perfect love.

2. Taking satan's advice and eating from the tree of the knowledge of good and evil not only set man up to make the same mistake he did, but also to take sides with him against love and thereby become vulnerable to him and his cosmos, which was based on his rebellion.

3. Under the shelter of God and His love in the Garden of Eden, man was covered, but by eating from the forbidden tree they came out from under this cover and became vulnerable to satan's cosmos.

4. Having left the world of love by their rebellion, the only alternative was satan's cosmos of darkness.

5. Thus man ceded his dominion over the earth to satan his new master.

The Fall Brought Satan's Judgment on Humanity and Their Planet

When satan rebelled and one third of the angels followed him in this violation of love, God was compelled by their actions to banish them from His world of love to what they had chosen, every form of rebellion against love—fear, condemnation, criticism, and confusion, and in the end eternal hell. This judgment was final, and there was no appeal (Matt. 25:41; 2 Pet. 2:4; Jude 6; Rev. 12:9). There is no room for the presence of these in love. Unfortunately, when Adam and Eve were deceived into emulating his example of rebellion against the love of God, they and their offspring brought the same condemnation upon themselves, "and the principle of death invaded their lives," as Grenz informs us.[21] This broke God's heart.

And so the judgment on satan was passed on to humanity and their planet. "Somehow it is not just man who has fallen but the whole created order along with him," wrote Torrance.[22] What appeared to them as a simple quest for more was in fact a lack of trust in God's love and provision. This resulted in their being expelled from the Garden of Eden and the tree of life within to live in a cursed, hostile world that, like them, groaned and travailed under the weight of it all and was busy dying. Accordingly, the judgment that would come in the end was foreshadowed everywhere by the absence of God's love, and the criticism and condemnation that arose out of their knowledge of good and evil and the perversion of it, in the immaterial and material world. As a result:

1. Satan and the angels that fell with him were judged for their conduct, and later when man made the same choice, they received the same judgment (Matt. 25:41).

2. Although Adam and Eve's expulsion from the Garden of Eden and the tree of life in its midst was a death sentence on them and all who would be born from their union, it was also an act of lovingkindness on God's part, because it kept them from being eternally estranged from Him.

3. Jesus said that all of mankind was condemned (John 3:18), referring to the judgment that was passed on Adam and Eve and their offspring through their rebellion in the garden.

4. But for the restraining presence of God's amazing grace working out His redemptive plans on earth, all would soon have been given over to satan's unlove and darkness without remedy.

The Fall Enabled Satan to Rob Man of His Superabundant Life and Fill Him with Fear unto Death

God made mankind to live forever and blessed them with superabundance. Their lives back then were easy, and they knew nothing but love and the pursuit of everything their hearts desired. They were full of life. They were healthy and strong, and there was no such thing as sickness or disease in that garden. Everything flourished. Truly heaven had come to earth, and nothing about this was supposed to change. They were meant to enjoy God's best forever. Peace and prosperity were the norm.

They were made in the image of God and had dominion over everything and were free to do anything they wanted, go anywhere they wished, and eat everything that they desired except the fruit of the tree of the knowledge of good and evil. This is how God planned life to be. It all showed off His lovingkindness. Who could have asked for anything more? And yet they did. What they asked for was the only thing God said they could not have, because God knew that it would ruin their perfect world of love and fill it with fear and death. Man did not take God's counsel to heart and disobeyed, setting in motion the most tragic events in human history.

Unfortunately this disobedience changed everything. Their "covering of glory was replaced by the nakedness of shame," stated Kline.[23] Out of mercy God expelled them from the garden and being able to eat from the tree of life, so that the tragic repercussions of their folly would not trap them in a world of unlove without the restoration of friendship with God and His love forever.

Thus they entered into a world of living and dying. This new experience must have been a terrifying shock to them. It reshaped everything. What had always glistened with life everywhere and in them began to age and die. Furthermore, this was hastened by pain, sorrow, and disease of every kind that is found in a world that has death in it. Fear, something they had never known before their folly, filled them and their world with negative options that had the potential to diminish and even shorten their lives. On that day, life was traded in for death, health for sickness, disease, and decay, superabundance for hard work and poverty, and worst of all, friendship with God for alienation, loneliness, unbearable frustration, and the vain search for love. Life became hard.

This was everything satan had hoped for. At last his loss became their loss also, and he set about to fill a world that was once covered in light with his darkness. This is what he has been doing in people, their families, and everything that means anything to them ever since (Eph. 2:1–3).

This has left mankind in conflict with God, themselves, and one another. Instead of love, man is marred by a suspicious, judgmental outlook that haunts his best intentions. Criticism has become too easy, and praise has become too hard. To enjoy God's fellowship once again the way it was in Eden, love must fill this world again.

Thank God, He had a plan for the restoration of man and his return to superabundance and sweet fellowship with Himself, which He had set in motion before the foundation of the world (Rev. 13:8; 1 Pet. 1:20; Eph. 1:4). It would be only a matter of time before God's Son would come to earth and put right all the wrongs. Then at last the curse would be reversed legally forever, and grace would take its place. Jesus is God's answer to this sick and dying world. His cross is the new rule believers live by today (Gal. 6:14–16).

Through Christ, friendship with God has been restored. The doors have been opened wide to every believer to be in health and prosper on every level even as their soul prospers in Christ, and live strong, healthy, superabundant lives full of love (3 John 2; John 10:10).

Christ's new creation lives by grace and is empowered to enjoy newness in the midst of the old, blessings surrounded by the world, and prosperity on every level while the world languishes in poverty and loss. But for the restraining influence of good churches, the Holy Spirit, and the angels, he would long ago have turned man and the world into chaos, darkness, and death.

Nevertheless, Jesus' triumph on the cross and His ensuing bodily resurrection three days later brought an end to satan's unbridled reign of fear and death, and thus ensured man's return to Eden on a new earth in the end for as many as believed (Eph. 1:15–23).

The empty cross turned everything around and became the rallying point for God's people (Gal. 6:14–18). It stopped satan's victory march across the world and cost him the right to accuse man before God, leaving him bound as a toothless lion to roam the earth, lying, stealing, accusing, and killing all he could before the end (John 8:44; 10:10; Rev. 12:10).

Once again the hope of eternal life and a personal relationship to God has been restored to man (Titus 1:2; 3:7), and they don't have to be afraid anymore. They are family now. Death's fearful tormentors have been silenced by Jesus Who said, "I am the resurrection and the life. He who believes in Me, though he may die, he shall live. And whoever lives and believes in Me shall never die" (John 11:25,26).

CHAPTER 3

Christ, the Second Adam

A New Creation

...Adam,...a type of Him who was to come.

Romans 5:14

Adam was the first man God created, and he was the father of us all. He and Eve were perfect in every way, and it was their destiny to reproduce and fill the earth with their offspring. As we all know, they failed in this when they ate of the forbidden fruit and derailed mankind's destiny to walk with God. Love then gave way to fear, and humanity has been tormented ever since, "exiled from the garden, shut out of the house, bombarded with noise instead of music," wrote N. T. Wright.[1] According to Rom. 5:14, Eph. 1:4, and Rev. 13:8, not only did God foresee the failure of the first creation, but He also planned all along on the birthing of a second creation through Christ, of Whom Adam and the first creation were the type. From the beginning there was hope.

Satan's handiwork has left the world in disarray. It no longer looks anything like the beautiful garden God planted so long ago. Gradually it has been slipping into more and more darkness as death continues to touch everything God spoke life into in the beginning. Contrary to what some say, this world and everything on it is not evolving into a better place. In spite of the fact that everything living is continually adapting to its changing surroundings as life strives to overcome, it is actually devolving. Nothing is as glorious as it was in the beginning, and although man's knowledge has certainly increased, this is even true of him. We have come a long way down since the day we were created in the image of God and had dominion over everything.

If this world could have outgrown its problems, there would have been no need for a Savior. Instead, the Scriptures speak of the foreknowledge of God and the necessity to plan the birth of a new creation through Christ, and new heavens and a new earth with the old one and everything on it burning up.

If God couldn't change this world to its former glory, then you can rest assured, neither can we. Nevertheless, man has come at it from every angle, by peaceful means and war, but to no avail in the long run. Satan's cosmos (world) is in his control, and man's finest attempts will always be quenched. At best, things may improve for a season, but the jaws of death that ever devour and are never satisfied soon take over. For this reason history is always repeating itself.

It is sheer vanity to think that we can permanently put right what God Himself cannot reverse. However, I am not denying the need to do our best as long as we never lose sight of the plans and purposes of God along the way.

> These all died in faith, not having received the promises, but having seen them afar off were assured of them, embraced them and confessed that they were strangers and pilgrims on the earth.
> For those who say such things declare plainly that they seek a homeland.
> And truly if they had called to mind that country from which they had come out, they would have had opportunity to return.
> But now they desire a better, that is, a heavenly country. Therefore God is not ashamed to be called their God, for He has prepared a city for them.
>
> *Heb. 11:13–16*

> For here we have no continuing city, but we seek the one to come.
>
> *Heb. 13:14*

God in His infinite wisdom realized that there would have to be a second Adam who would birth a new humanity that would not be vulnerable to satan's temptation, on a new earth in a new universe, having banished satan and his followers forever to a place of punishment and isolation.

The coming of Jesus Christ is about God starting all over again through the plan of redemption and the message of salvation to restore man's fellowship with Him. And Jesus, God's only begotten Son, is the One Whom He chose to accomplish this task.

> But when the fullness of the time had come, God sent forth His Son, born of a woman, born under the law, to redeem those who were under the law, that we might receive the adoption as sons.
> And because you are sons, God has sent forth the Spirit of His Son into your hearts, crying out, "Abba, Father!" Therefore you are no longer a slave but a son, and if a son, then an heir of God through Christ.
>
> *Gal. 4:4–7 (John 3:16)*

In summation, humanity was irreparably marred by the fall. Things would never be the same again because unlove had polluted everything and changed the nature of man, which would remain this way until the new birth. His instincts were no longer love, and the only way out for him was for God to create a new humanity through His Son (Eph. 2:13); hence, as I have already stated, He established His plans to birth a new creation through Christ. the second Adam. This is why the Scriptures speak of Adam as a type of Christ. What the first Adam failed to do, the second Adam successfully accomplished: the creation of a new humanity by the Spirit that would live triumphant lives of love empowered by Christ's grace (Rom. 5), awaiting the return of their Lord and Savior.

Jesus Was the First of a New Humanity

1. **Jesus is the second Adam, who became a life-giving spirit.**

> And so it is written, *"The first man Adam became a living being."* The last Adam became a **life-giving spirit**.
> However, the spiritual is not first, but the natural, and afterward the spiritual.
> The first man was of the earth, made of dust; the second Man is the Lord from heaven.
> As was the man of dust, so also are those who are made of dust; and as is the heavenly Man, so also are those who are heavenly.
> And as we have borne the image of the man of dust, we shall also bear the image of the heavenly Man.
>
> *1 Cor. 15:45–49*

2. **Jesus was the first of the new humanity to rise from the dead.**

first—*prōtos* (first in time or place; first in rank)

"that the Christ would suffer, that He would be the **first** to rise from the dead, and would proclaim light to the Jewish people and to the Gentiles."

Acts 26:23 (Rev. 2:8)

3. **Jesus after His resurrection was the prototype of a new humanity.**

firstborn—*prōtotokos* (firstborn; prototype)

For whom He foreknew, He also predestined to be conformed to the image of His Son, that He might be the **firstborn** among many brethren.

Rom. 8:29
(Col. 1:15,18; Heb. 1:6; Rev. 1:5)

4. **Jesus after His resurrection was the firstfruits of the promised harvest.**

firstfruits—*aparchē* (firstfruits, first of the harvest; firstling, beginning of the sacrifice)

But now Christ is risen from the dead, and has become the **firstfruits** of those who have fallen asleep.
For since by man came death, by Man also came the resurrection of the dead.
For as in Adam all die, even so in Christ all shall be made alive.

But each one in his own order: Christ the **firstfruits**, afterward those who are Christ's at His coming.

1 Cor. 15:20–23

5. **Jesus was the first of the new humanity to pioneer the way.**

forerunner—*prodromos* (forerunner; precursor)

This hope we have as an anchor of the soul, both sure and steadfast, and which enters the Presence behind the veil,
where the **forerunner** has entered for us, even Jesus, having become High Priest forever according to the order of Melchizedek.

Heb. 6:19,20

6. **Jesus has become the author of eternal salvation for the new humanity.**

captain, author—*archēgos* (author, founder, prince, ruler, originator; first cause)

For it was fitting for Him, for whom are all things and by whom are all things, in bringing many sons to glory, to make the **captain** of their salvation perfect through sufferings.

Heb. 2:10 (Acts 3:15; 5:31; Heb. 12:2)
(Heb. 5:9, "author"=aitios—source, cause)

7. **Jesus has made this new humanity one new man in Himself.**

> having abolished in His flesh the enmity, that is, the law of commandments contained in ordinances, so as to create **in Himself one new man** from the two, thus making peace,
>
> *Eph. 2:15 (Rom. 5:15–19)*

8. **Jesus has formed a new creation in Himself.**

> Therefore, if anyone is **in Christ**, he is a **new creation**; old things have passed away; behold, all things have become new.
>
> *2 Cor. 5:17 (Gal. 6:15)*

9. **Jesus will come again to receive His new humanity in the resurrection and give them new bodies like His, and live with them forever in the new heavens and new earth.**

> Beloved, now we are children of God; and it has not yet been revealed what we shall be, but we know that when He is revealed, **we shall be like Him**, for we shall see Him as He is.
>
> *1 John 3:2 (1 Cor. 15:42–49)*

A New Humanity

Therefore, from the beginning God promised man a Savior who would come and restore all things (Acts 3:19–21). When everything had been made ready, the first part of this plan was implemented. God sent His Son to live perfectly before them by the love they had lost in the Garden of Eden, to reveal Himself to them once again (John 14:7–11; 17:1–26).

Jesus was full of grace and truth (John 1:14–18). There was "a match between his life and his speech," wrote Allan Coppedge, and He "was a living model of what God wants us to understand."[2] At the age of 33, He offered Himself up as the perfect sacrifice for all sin, and on the cross, which Newbigin called "the central unveiling of the infinite love of God,"[3] He showed off the love of God as never seen before on earth, triumphing over satan and his reign of fear. Truly He was proven to be the Friend that sticks closer than a brother (Prov. 18:24). The cross revealed God's attitude towards sin and sinners—He loves everyone unconditionally and died to save them and their world. There was no other way to accomplish this (John 14:6; Acts 4:12). He gave them back the love they lost in the garden.

With the coming of Christ and His triumph on the cross, humanity received a new opportunity to walk with God as they await Christ's return in the end and the consummation of all things. Wright describes this as "the recreation of humankind through the life-giving activity of the final Adam, whose image will be borne by all who belong to him."[4] As Grenz emphasizes, Jesus is "the New Human, the New Adam, the founder of a new humanity, the fountainhead of a new order of human beings."[5]

Therefore, it is correct to say that Jesus after His resurrection was the first of a new humanity destined for the eternals, and that we who believe are included in that number.

Jesus Is the Prototype of a New Humanity
(Gk. *prōtotokos*—firstborn)

> For whom He foreknew, He also predestined to be conformed to the image of His Son, that He might be the **firstborn** among many brethren.
>
> *Rom. 8:29*

> He is the image of the invisible God, the **firstborn** over all creation.
>
> *Col. 1:15*

> And He is the head of the body, the church, who is the beginning, the **firstborn** from the dead, that in all things He may have the preeminence.
>
> *Col. 1:18*

> and from Jesus Christ, the faithful witness, the **firstborn** from the dead, and the ruler over the kings of the earth. To Him who loved us and washed us from our sins in His own blood,
>
> *Rev. 1:5*

Thus the victory of Christ and His cross is the new wisdom of God that we triumphantly live by (1 Cor. 1:22–24, 30; Eph. 3:8–12; Gal. 6:14–16). It has become the reason for every believer's joy. Its triumphant message is the good news the world needs to hear. It has enabled God to make you and everything you care about brand new, and suit you by grace to live with Him forever on a new earth in new heavens full of love.

In light of the biblical record of what Christ accomplished on the cross, it behooves us to have a fresh discussion on what it means to become a Christian. The whole idea that they are little more than a spiritual branch of social do-gooders is brought into serious question by the biblical teaching of Paul that Christ has birthed a new creation that belongs to the coming eternal age, of which He became the prototype at His bodily resurrection.

Even Jesus taught that His followers would be rejected by society and become outcasts (John 15:18,19). It would appear that there is a real, substantive difference between non-Christians and Christians. It is not merely emotional or philosophical. It is actual. It is spiritual. According to the new creation message, a real change has taken place in believers. They have been born from above (John 3:3) and suited for eternity. He was the light of the world, and they are called to reflect the same glorious light.

This is why the Holy Scriptures speak of "Adam, who is a type of Him who was to come" (Rom. 5:14), and Jesus as the second Adam. Truly He was the first of a new humanity to come that would receive the promises forfeited by the old. By the way, this is also why the Apostle Paul spoke of those Corinthian church members as a "new creation" in Him (2 Cor. 5:17).

In the words of James D. G. Dunn, "Paul perceives Christ as the image of the Creator, that is, the image God intended for humanity. Salvation is the completion of the original goal of creation—to renew that image, to bring humanity to that fuller share of divine glory which Adam forfeited."[6] And E. Earle Ellis explains, "From the Creation narratives Paul draws a typological relation between Adam and Christ in which the whole scope of cosmic redemption appears to be encompassed: *[En Christō]* a man enters a new resurrection creation (*[kainē ktisis]*) whose head and sovereign is the Lord Christ; and from Rom. 8 it appears that the whole cosmic order is to be in this new redeemed creation.…Both head a new creation; but where Adam's failure brought sin and death to all *[en Adam]*, Christ's victory brought righteousness and immortal life to all *[en Christō]*."[7]

Make no mistake about it, Christians are not a cleaned-up version of the old creation. By the Spirit they have been made new from the inside out. They are a counterculture, "a renewed way of living within the present"[8] and "the beginning of what is to come,"[9] as John Howard Yoder wrote. Grace has saved them and empowered them to return to love and a personal relationship to God. They are the promised, end-time, new people of God who live by a new rule—the cross. For them it is more than a symbol; it is the power that overcame the old world and established a new one foreshadowing the eternal age to come (Gal. 6:14–16).

Believers Are a New Creation Suited for New Heavens and a New Earth

> Therefore, if anyone is in Christ, he is a new creation; old things have passed away; behold, all things have become new.
>
> *2 Cor. 5:17*

> For in Christ Jesus neither circumcision nor uncircumcision avails anything, but a new creation.
>
> *Gal. 6:15*

> "And to the angel of the church of the Laodiceans write, 'These things says the Amen, the Faithful and True Witness, the Beginning of the creation of God:'"
>
> *Rev. 3:14*

For we know that if our earthly house, this tent, is destroyed, we have a building from God, a house not made with hands, eternal in the heavens.
For in this we groan, earnestly desiring to be clothed with our habitation which is from heaven,
if indeed, having been clothed, we shall not be found naked.
For we who are in this tent groan, being burdened, not because we want to be unclothed, but further clothed, that mortality may be swallowed up by life.
Now He who has prepared us for this very thing is God, who also has given us the Spirit as a guarantee.

2 Cor. 5:1–5

Nevertheless we, according to His promise, look for new heavens and a new earth in which righteousness dwells.

2 Pet. 3:13

For the earnest expectation of the creation eagerly waits for the revealing of the sons of God.
For the creation was subjected to futility, not willingly, but because of Him who subjected it in hope;
because the creation itself also will be delivered from the bondage of corruption into the glorious liberty of the children of God.
For we know that the whole creation groans and labors with birth pangs together until now.

Rom. 8:19–22

> Of His own will He brought us forth by the word of truth, that we might be a kind of firstfruits of His creatures.
>
> *Jas. 1:18*
>
> *Note: Eph. 4:24; Col. 3:10*

This new creation has always been God's dream, and it has become the hope of His people; however, it wasn't until the New Testament writers, especially Paul, explained the details of the fellowship of the mystery of Christ that had been hidden from the beginning, and plainly presented Him as the firstfruits of the new creation and the door to fellowship with God, that Christians began to understand the fullness of the message (Eph. 3).

Thus the New Testament explains the Old Testament and makes sense out of its messianic promises. As the Scriptures remind us, all the promises are fulfilled, "yes, yes, and amen," in Him (2 Cor. 1:19,20). This was Paul's way of expressing his confidence in Jesus as the Promised One. As Eduard Schweizer put it, "God…said Yes to us in Jesus. This is such a miracle for Paul that he can conceive of it only as a new creation, as an entirely new world which God has prepared for us."[10]

This has brought the days of ethnic preference to an end and opened the door to everyone, regardless of their background, to know God personally. The mystery of Christ is about fellowship and the bringing together of all believers, regardless of their ethnic background, into communities of love known today as churches (Eph. 3:10). Christ has brought believing Jews and Gentiles together in one body—His (Eph. 2:14–22; Col. 3:10,11). They are the true elect Israel of God (Gal. 6:15,16).

As we have seen, some authors have gone so far as to speak of Christians as a counterculture. Though this may seem a little radical, it is true. When Jesus said He would build, or gather together, His own assembly apart from national Israel, He was saying just that (Matt. 16:18). In fact, when He said, "Render to Caesar what is Caesar's, and to God what is God's," (Matt. 22:21) He was bolstering the idea of a new and separate people living in the midst of the old: "Honor the civil government and honor the kingdom of God." Of course, this is not an abdication of our responsibility to make a substantive contribution to society for the good of all so that we might live in peace and prosperity (1 Tim. 2:1–2).

Nevertheless, as John reminds us in his Gospel, it is also true that Jesus said to His Father, "I have given them Your word; and the world has hated them because they are not of the world, just as I am not of the world" (John 17:14–16). It was about Christians and their loving relationships in their churches that He said, "...that they may be made perfect [through love] in one, and that the world may know that You have sent Me and have loved them as You have loved Me" (John 17:20–26).

Christian, the Spirit of God has turned you into a new you—a sanctified (separated unto God) one who belongs to God—so you should not see yourself any other way.

Getting saved makes believers something new that has never been seen on earth before, and yet, as we have noted, was already on God's heart from the beginning. In fact, Paul was quite comfortable in his epistles with speaking about who they were and who they have become in terms of dead versus alive (Eph. 2:1–7), old versus new (2 Cor. 5:17), flesh versus Spirit (Rom. 8:1–13), and those who have died with Christ and risen with Him (Rom. 6:5–11; Col. 2:12,13; 3:1). He goes so far as to say that their lives are quite literally hidden with Christ in God (Col. 3:3) with a new access to every spiritual blessing that is theirs today in Christ in the heavens (Eph. 1:3). These are only a sampling of the ways in which Paul explicitly describes the real differences that exist between the lost and the saved.

Thus Christ has birthed a new humanity through grace that is empowered by the Spirit from within to show off the fellowship of God's love in their churches and reveal the coming glory after the resurrection in the end when the glory church in heaven today will cover the earth. "In other words, we are called to the life of the *New Creation*," wrote William Manson. "Yet not in the sense of envisaging a purely future goal, but…in the sense that we already possess through Christ the gifts of the World to Come."[11]

The Gospel of the Kingdom

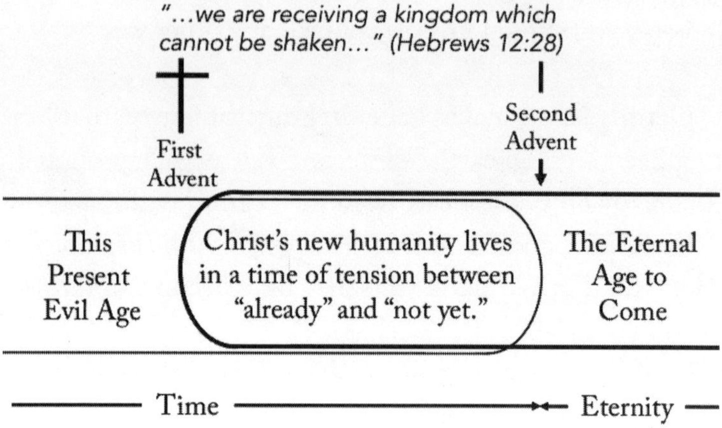

Beginning at the cross, God's new creation inherited the dominion lost by Adam, and it is their destiny to rule victoriously where satan once ruled unchallenged, and grace is their enabler (Rom. 5:17). We now live under the dominion of Christ, as L. S. Thornton so thoroughly presented in his book of that very title.[12] Since the cross satan has been rendered a toothless, noisy lion that all Christians can overcome at will because of the blood of Jesus (1 Pet. 5:8,9; Rev. 12:11). This was one of the reasons Jesus said that the gates of hell would not prevail against the church (Matt. 16:18). "Christians, therefore, have entered through the Christ into the New Age," declares Manson, and "...are already conscious of tasting the powers of the World to Come."[13]

Satan's Cosmos Is in Disarray, and He Has Been Restrained

The days of satan's dominance are over. Since the cross, his wounds have been carrying out a death sentence in him. He has been exposed for the condemned liar, thief, and murderer that he is (John 8:44; 10:10). Jesus has overcome the world he runs (John 16:33). Today Jesus reigns as Lord over satan and everything demonic on our behalf (John 12:31; Eph. 1:19–23; 1 Pet. 3:22). In this sense he has been bound for a season (2 Thess. 2:7–12; Rev. 20:2).

Today through faith in our authority to use Jesus' name, the least of us can overcome the devil and his wiles; furthermore, we can undo his evil works (Mark 16:17,18; Acts 3:16; Luke 10:17–20). Believers have been called to embrace the triumph of Christ over him as their own. We need to reorientate our thinking to line up with this new power over satan and his demons. Nothing need hold us back anymore. We have won through Christ's victory. Take dominion! Christ's new creation has been given back humanity's lost authority.

Thank God, satan has been banished from God's presence and can no longer legally accuse us before Him. Jesus has justified us forever. Thus his powers have been limited for a season, and he lives in fear of the authority of Christ's new creation churches. Today we are citizens of the coming kingdom of peace, and none of us need heed that toothless lion anymore (1 Pet. 5:8,9). We are free to live by love, and "to live from that love means to stand in the freedom of a Christian," wrote Ernst Käsemann.[14] Fellowship with God has been restored to man. Our daily prayer is, "Your kingdom come. Your will be done on earth as it is in heaven" (Matt. 6:10).

A New Heart for Christ's New Creation

When the first Adam turned away from God's counsel, his heart followed suit, and mankind has been adrift ever since. Over the years our hearts have degenerated, and along with this our consciences have become selfish and subjective. Who knows the extent of what we have lost since the day we were created in the image of God. The prophet Jeremiah concluded about living in Law Covenant days, "The heart is deceitful above all things, and desperately wicked (incurably sick); who can know it?" (Jer. 17:9). For unbelievers, true love has become foreign to them; nevertheless, this has not stopped them from vainly trying to pursue it. It seems that God left something inside us after the fall that yearns to be satisfied by true love and peace—a renewed relationship with Him.

While the eternal age is yet to come, with all its promised glories on a new earth where man will quite literally walk with God and, as Job prophesied, see Him face to face with their own eyes (Job 19:25–27), many of its promises are available in part to believers in this Dispensation of

Grace today. With the coming of the Holy Spirit, these last days have seen the dawning of what is yet to come in full when Christ returns. A new heart for believers with the indwelling presence of the Holy Spirit in their lives is a partial taste of these things. This was foretold in the Old Testament: "I will give you a new heart and put a new spirit within you; I will take the heart of stone out of your flesh and give you a heart of flesh" (Ezek. 36:26). It was fulfilled in the New Testament (Heb. 8:10–12; 10:16,17). Thus Christ's new creation has been prequalified to live by God's love and enjoy a new relationship with Him before the end when He returns.

The glories to come have dawned (John 17). What amazing times we live in! Thank God for our newness in Christ. Believers have a new heart, and they need to learn how to live with this newness. Peter said that this was central to the Gospel message that he preached (1 Pet. 1:22–25). Here is a translation of 1 Pet. 1:22,23 by Mark Dubis in his book *I Peter: A Handbook on the Greek Text*:[15]

> Since you have purified yourselves by obeying the truth in order that you might show sincere brotherly love, love one another ongoingly from a pure heart because you have been born again not by a perishable seed, but by an imperishable one, namely, through the perpetually enduring word of God.

These scriptures speak of believers having purified hearts—being born again so that they can have sincere love for one another. The phrase "have purified" is in the perfect tense, which means that it is a one-time occurrence with continuing effect. Believer, you have a new, purified heart, and it's there to stay. Don't allow satan to downplay its value and fill it with his nonsense, because you know he is going to attempt to do so (Acts 5:3). Walk in your newness and guard it.

In his commentary on *1 Peter*, Paul J. Achtemeier's translation of these verses reminds us that the goal of the Gospel message "is unfeigned mutual love."[16] Allow this to always fill your new heart.

Christian, you really do have a new heart; as I said before, the old one (Jer. 17:9) has been replaced (Ezek. 36:26; Heb. 8:10–12; 10:16,17). Furthermore, the idea some have that Christians are two-natured beings (old heart/new heart) who can never be sure who they really are is monstrous. Christian, you do have a flesh, but make no mistake about it, your flesh is no longer you; it is a voice from the grave that died with Christ.

Believers have only one nature, and it is as new as the resurrected Christ Himself. We don't have a second nature—the bad us. We do have a flesh that is not us. Yes, the Scriptures do speak of an old man (Rom. 6:6; Eph. 4:22; Col. 3:9), a flesh (Rom. 7:18; 8:1), that is an unwanted, resident evil that Paul taught is no longer us. So why make the mistake of calling it a second nature, seeing it is no longer you? I look like Christ on the inside; that was enough for Paul, and it is enough for me. That the new me is always challenged by the old me is a non-issue unless I choose to make it otherwise.

Christian, you are a new creation in Christ, and you have a flesh that is no longer you (Rom. 7:17–20). Your flesh will yet be transformed in the resurrection in the end and made perfect to be compatible with who you already are in Christ. In the meantime there is no taming it or changing it much or reforming it. It is dead and buried with Christ, and as Paul said, "It is no longer I…, but sin that dwells in me" (Rom. 7:20). Treat it that way. It is not the new you. There is not one scripture in the Holy Bible that tells us to do anything but see it as crucified, count it as dead, ignore it, and don't corrupt it any further (Rom. 6:11–23; 8:12,13; Gal. 6:7,8), and know no one after the flesh (2 Cor. 5:16). You cannot change your flesh permanently, and God knows this better than you (John 6:63). And by the way, the problem of temptation is common to every Christian's flesh (1 Cor. 10:13). Thank God for the abundant grace and righteousness that empower us to reign in life through Jesus (Rom. 5:17) and feel good all the time about our new selves. This is very big, and until you catch on to the new creation understanding of your position in grace, you will remain unstable. Don't be double-minded about your newness and how good you look all the time because of grace alone.

My New Creation Declaration

I do not have a "dark side!" Nowhere does the Holy Bible say that I have an old nature to reform and a new nature to develop. Certainly I have a new nature and a flesh that is carnal; in other words, it belongs to the old me before I was saved, but (1) it is no longer I, (2) it has been crucified with Christ, (3) I count it as dead, buried, and forgotten, and (4) I have no command in the Holy Scriptures to improve it. However, this does not mean I have dual natures. I only have one nature, and it is new and as righteous as Christ Himself. The old is dead, having died with Christ, and I am alive, having risen with Him. I am new, new, new forevermore, thanks to marvelous, intoxicating grace.

Grasp this so that you never misunderstand yourself or others again, and guilt no longer overshadows your judgment for all the wrong reasons. Thank God, our standing is in grace by the Spirit, and not in our fleshly righteousness or unrighteousness. The cross crucified "business as usual" for believers and gave them a new way of interpreting life. Thank God for His Son's righteousness by grace alone.

Christian, you are new in the Spirit (2 Cor. 5:17; Rom. 7:6), and the wise choice is to embrace this newness and walk in it by faith (Gal. 5:25). Talk about it and not the old.

Beware of embracing the memories of who you were before you were saved, and walking in your flesh that is no longer you. By the way, this would be living a lie.

Paul called this kind of wrong thinking and believing "still carnal" (1 Cor. 3:3)—the way they were before they were saved. Furthermore, today believers have the power, love, and sound mind of the Holy Spirit to enable them to run with who they are in Christ (2 Tim. 1:7). They don't think beyond what is written (1 Cor. 4:6). We have new creation parameters.

As far as Paul was concerned, Christians are a new humanity. To bolster this he insisted that they no longer consider one another the way they were in their flesh before they were saved, which he said by the Spirit had "passed away." They were to see one another as "new" (2 Cor. 5:16,17). Paul was either exaggerating the point he was trying to make or affirming something very real that had happened to them since they believed, which is what we evangelicals insist he was doing by the Spirit of revelation.

What Does It Mean to Become a Christian?

Christ's triumph has restored the possibility of having a personal, unconditional relationship with God once again by making believers brand new. Through the gift of His righteousness by grace, the Spirit of God has formed a new humanity like Christ their Forerunner, suited for new heavens and a new earth. The journey forward with God has been restored. It is now possible for people to be translated from satan's present kingdom of darkness (world) to Christ's eternal kingdom of light (world) (Col. 1:13). This is what getting saved is all about. Christ's new creation has been invited to live in God's "unapproachable light" (1 Tim. 6:16) before the resurrection in the end. Today believers are "light-walkers."

Those steeped in the extreme European traditions of Christianity, both Roman and Protestant, have often lost sight of this. Far too often they live by a medieval, short-sighted theology that is drenched in sin and not grace. Thus they either minimize the free, direct access to God believers enjoy by grace, or legalize it to the point of falling from grace. In both instances the freedom and friendship that Christ paid so dear a price to restore has been sufficiently obscured to turn Christianity from relationship to ritual. In many cases this has become a turn-off to people needing real answers. It has created an open door for the accuser of the brethren (Rev. 12:10) to once again open his big, unwelcome mouth and make good, sincere believers feel bad about themselves and others. There is no freedom in this, only bondage.

Christians Belong to Christ's Spiritual Kingdom, Not Satan's Defeated System

It is also imperative to understand that the Christian message isn't another way to prop up society with a positive affirmation system. The world system is run by satan and is a doomed system. It has been overcome by Christ (John 16:33; 1 John 5:4,5), and a new spiritual kingdom has been set up by Him in the midst of the old. They are parallel kingdoms that never converge. Christ's new creation churches are custodians of the kingdom of light (Eph. 3:21; 1 Tim. 3:15).

Our message isn't about social reformation, although we are all for it and will do anything by the Spirit to help bring it to pass. Nevertheless, our goal is not "the moral chaperoning of the whole culture," as Yoder stated;[17] it is about the offer of a spiritual transformation that God wants to perform in everyone's life to empower them to live by love. This is called getting saved or born again by the Spirit. And those who have experienced this spiritual transformation have the grand opportunity of renewing their minds with the promises of the Word to suit them for their citizenship in Christ's new creation movement centered in their churches. In fact, "through Christ,...Christians are even now sharing in the life and worship of the world to come," declares R. J. McKelvey.[18]

[18] *The New Temple* by R. J. McKelvey (1969), p. 154. By permission of Oxford University Press.

The world is in trouble. The Scriptures warn all who are not saved that their lives are being influenced regularly by demonic forces that run the world from behind the scenes. It says that the people of the world walk "according to the course of this world [satan's system], according to the prince of the power of the air, the spirit that now works in the sons of disobedience, among whom also we all once conducted ourselves in the lusts of our flesh, fulfilling the desires of the flesh and of the mind, and were by nature children of wrath, just as the others" (Eph. 2:2,3). In the same epistle, referring to the complex system of control, or as Walter Wink calls it, the "Domination System"[19] that satan has put in place to manipulate God's creation, Paul said, "For we do not wrestle against flesh and blood, but against principalities, against powers, against the rulers of the darkness of this age, against spiritual hosts of wickedness in the heavenly places" (Eph. 6:12; 1:21).

This is a far cry from the love that once ruled the world and those in it; nevertheless, Christ's new humanity has overcome through the cross. The second Adam has made it possible for mankind to be saved from this world system and return to fellowship with God, because "through his reconciling life and atoning passion he brought the love and power of God to bear upon its deep-seated disorder so as to make an end of it for ever," wrote Torrance.[20] In fact, the Scriptures tell us that He has the power to translate man from satan's kingdom of darkness to His kingdom of light (Col. 1:9–14), or to bring about what Robert C. Tannehill calls "release from the old dominion and transfer to the new."[21] Furthermore, Yoder reminds us, "This creation of the one new humanity is itself the purpose that God had in all ages, is itself the 'mystery,' the gospel now to be proclaimed."[22] The cross devastated satan's plans (Col. 2:11–15). Because of this we now have a new world (cosmic) outlook on life. This is also why our churches and homes are so important to us. They are a part of something new. They belong to the future.

Because of Christ's sacrifice on the cross, this new humanity has been forgiven of all sin and given the gift of His righteousness to stand in by grace for the rest of their lives. Furthermore, they have been empowered by the Holy Spirit, Whom He sent to take His place, to reign triumphantly in life as they live by love in their churches once again in fellowship with their God (Heb. 8; 10). Thus Christ has given a new identity to the saved. In fact, as the Scriptures put it, they are hidden with Christ in God (Col. 3:3). Everything about them has taken on a new complexion. Whereas they have been birthed physically in Adam, they have now been birthed spiritually in Christ the second Adam.

This is one of the reasons the Holy Scriptures speak of Jesus after His resurrection and exaltation to His Father's right hand as "the Beginning of the creation of God" (Rev. 3:14), and His brother James reminds us that it was "of His own will He brought us forth by the word of truth, that we might be a kind of firstfruits of His creatures" (Jas. 1:18). Paul, the apostle to the Gentiles, says to the Corinthian church, "You are new creation," and he concludes about the life they had before they were saved with these words: "Old things have passed away; behold, all things have become new" (2 Cor. 5:17).

What this actually means is this: the real Christian message isn't about social reorientation but rather about a spiritual regeneration that is so powerful that God can take ordinary people like you and me and remake them from the inside out into a brand new creation by forgiving them of all their sins, taking out their old, hard hearts (Jer. 17:9), giving them new, soft ones (Heb. 8:10–12; 10:16,17), and putting His Spirit in them to stay.

Who you have become in Christ is the new, authentic self Christians are called to walk in by faith, and what Jesus would look like if He were in their place on earth. William Manson went so far as to describe this as "a union or interfusion of personalities. Christ is the new *Ego* of the Christian, and the Head or informing principle of the new humanity."[23] For Adam, being a human being was all about him. For Christ's new humanity, it is all about who they have become in Him.

Your new authentic self is:

1. **Who you are in Christ** = my new self (*identity*) (Col. 2:6–15)

2. **Who Christ is in you** = my new lifestyle (*testimony*) (Col. 3:10,11; Eph. 3)

By overlooking these profound truths, some have inadvertently minimized the new creation message. Doing so has weakened how they see themselves. Christian, right now you are who you are in Christ and not who you were in the flesh before you were saved and received the Spirit. This is tremendous! You are complete in Him (Col. 2:10). It is how God sees you, and satan will do all he can to keep you from seeing yourself this way. It is who you are, and the devil doesn't want you to know it. Grace has made this possible. We live by a new norm—Jesus.

Bad thinking produces bad believing, and together they make for bad living. Too many believers live weak lives under the circumstances and in bondage to the falsehood that they still are (by nature) the person they were before they were saved. This is nonsense, against the Scripture record. Speaking of this truth contained in Paul and Timothy's letter to the Colossian church, Brian Habig and Les Newsom wrote, "They prayed for a profound change in *thinking* that would lead to a profound change in *living*. Apparently, believers are changed from the inside out as their thinking changes" (Col. 1:9–12).[24] Thus they get to catch up, as it were, with who they already are in Christ.

The wrong kind of thinking kept me in bondage to my past problems for many years long after I was in the ministry. It made me a victim of everything I had ever been through and kept me weak. It made me feel and look like a hypocrite. It gave my flesh the excuse it needed to remain in control, and my enemies the opportunity they sought to malign me. The day God opened my eyes to who I already was in Christ through grace, and how powerful I was in the Spirit, my chains fell off, and I was a free man. All I had to do was walk away and, with the support of my peers and our church's deliverance ministry, overcome the bondages in my flesh. Thank God for grace and the freedom in our churches to do so in a loving environment of acceptance and praise. Jesus and His cross are our mutual place of glorying, and not our crucified and dead flesh.

Thereafter, what I had to do was reorientate my thinking to all the advantages of the new creation message and learn to walk in who I already was by faith, "the Lord's freedman" (1 Cor. 7:22). When you know who you are regardless of the noise your flesh is making, and that it is no longer you, walking in the Spirit is not only desirable but also very powerful and rewarding. The devil has gained much space in our lives because of incorrect thinking, and he is the only one who is happy with this arrangement. No wonder the ill-informed spend so much time trying to counsel the flesh and so little on prophetic ministry—edification, exhortation, and comfort (1 Cor. 14:3)—building up the new you.

Through grace, it is now possible to return to love and be empowered by the Spirit of God to share with the world our fellowship with Him and one another through our churches and their outreach of love as they make disciples to the four corners of the earth (Matt. 28:18–20; Mark 16:15; Acts 1:8). Mark Dever reminds us that in our churches we provide "a visual presentation of the gospel when we forgive one another as Christ has forgiven us, when we commit to one another as Christ has committed to us, and when we lay down our lives for one another as Christ laid down his life for us."[25]

Believers are new, and they live by the word of faith, drawing from the resources of the Holy Spirit within and not their flesh. Their churches in a very real sense are outposts of heaven on earth, foreshadowing what will one day fill the earth in the end upon Christ's return (Gal. 2:20; Jas. 1:18; John 17). They belong to the coming new age when God and man will be one again through love.

The New Creation's Hope

The final stage of the plan of salvation begins after the resurrection in the end and the great judgment, when the lost will be condemned along with satan and his angels to the eternal lake of fire, never to trouble Christ's new humanity ever again. It is then that the saved will receive their rewards, and God will re-create the world and the universe anew and become all in all with His people the way it was in Eden. "In the final consummation of God's loving purpose," wrote Newbigin, "we and all creation will be caught up into the perfect rapture of that mutual love which is the life of God Himself."[26] His love will then fill everything and everyone who is in Christ (Eph. 1:3–12; 1 Cor. 15:20–28).

At last the Lamb and His bride will be one, and there will be feasting, celebration and the promised oneness between God and man as His love fills everything and everyone—pleasures at His right hand forevermore (Psa. 16:11). What a happy marriage! What a perfect ending! Or should I say beginning? Thus the plan of salvation will have accomplished the purposes of God, and His creation will have returned to Eden's bliss. The second Adam will have triumphed where the first Adam failed, and His inheritance in the new creation will have come to full fruition (Eph. 1:15–22). What a safe place! What a time of endless pleasures at the right hand of God!

This is why the plan of salvation is a faith message based on Christ's victory on the cross alone, and why God calls those who believe this to repent (change their minds) and turn from their old master the devil, and by faith receive Jesus Christ as their Lord and Savior from sin (unlove) and be restored to fellowship with Him. As Manson explains, "[I]t is not apart from but in fellowship with [Jesus] that repentance, the turning from self to God, the putting of God first, the recognizing that one has *no future except God*," is to be brought about.[27] Getting saved equals getting back in fellowship with God through Christ.

CHAPTER 4

Back to Eden and the Good Life

With Shouts of "Grace, Grace!"

The Dispensation of Grace has opened the door to everything the Jews longed for in their prophetic future. What we enjoy today as Christians is the commencement of what they dreamed about for themselves and their families, though they didn't know the details prior to the coming of Christ and the revelation of this mystery by Paul (Eph. 3:1–13). Truly Christ's new humanity are proven to be the heirs of the Jewish promises and their restoration to full sonship with God by grace alone (Gal. 4).

> Of this salvation the prophets have inquired and searched carefully, who prophesied of the grace that would come to you,
> searching what, or what manner of time, the Spirit of Christ who was in them was indicating when He testi-

> fied beforehand the sufferings of Christ and the glories that would follow.
> To them it was revealed that, not to themselves, but to us they were ministering the things which now have been reported to you through those who have preached the gospel to you by the Holy Spirit sent from heaven—things which angels desire to look into.
>
> *1 Pet. 1:10–12*

Everything about Christianity is what God promised Abraham for the Jews and the Gentiles; no wonder Paul called believers "the Israel of God" (Gal. 6:16). The Dispensation of Grace lies at the heart of the mystery of the fellowship of Christ that was hidden from Old Testament saints about the day of salvation, which would open the door to all believers to enjoy fellowship with God together in Christ's churches, as revealed by Paul (Eph. 3), and later on after the end in the glory church that would fill the new earth. Then and only then would the conflict between good and evil be over, and the lamb and the lion would lie down together. It rendered the Old Covenant promises fulfilled. This is the victory of grace.

Looking back, the introduction of the Jewish law written in stone brought God's people's awareness of good and evil to new heights. In fact, it rubbed their noses in the smelly fact that living by the knowledge of good and evil was a killer. No wonder that administration was known as an administration of condemnation (2 Cor. 3:9), bondage (Gal. 4:24,25), and even death (2 Cor. 3:7).

For Old Testament Jews, the law was a bondage, but Christ has set us free from that bondage (Heb. 2:14,15). Jesus said their yoke was heavy, and our yoke today is easy in comparison (Matt. 11:28–30; 23:4). Friendship with God has been restored. The hope of returning to Eden's joy has been secured for us by grace. Once again man can live by love alone, empowered by the Spirit within. This is the key difference. Believers today know God personally, and it is all thanks to grace.

Moses' Law Administration vs. Christ's Grace Administration

We know that the law was not implemented to save man (Gal. 3:19; Heb. 10:1–3), but to preserve and sanctify a nation to God for His purposes. Technically it was for that time and that purpose alone, although it ever remains good (Rom. 7:16; 1 Tim. 1:5–11) and the foundation on which this dispensation of living by love through grace has been built. The Jewish nation enabled God to record and sustain the lineage of Christ all the way up until Jesus' miraculous birth in Bethlehem. In other words, John Wilmot mentions, "The people who sprang from Abraham through Isaac and Jacob, called Israel, were favored to be the means but not the end."[1] It was Jesus who would bring grace and truth to new levels by establishing a dispensation or administration of grace, if you please, that would prepare a people who, along with the saints who had gone before them, would populate a new planet Earth. Only then in the end would the whole story of the grace of God that has brought salvation to mankind and his world be fully realized (2 Pet. 3:10–13).

The Jewish nation was a people of the flesh who prided themselves in their physical lineage. Today we believers are a people of the Spirit who glory in the cross and our inclusion in the greatest lineage of all—God's heavenly family in Christ Jesus. For the Jews it was their physical ties to Abraham, Isaac, Jacob, etc., and they took care to trace their family lines back to those three. Today, although we certainly do enjoy spiritual ties to Abraham, we only glory in the cross (Gal. 6:12–16), and every one of us is just as careful to trace our new family line back to Three—Father, Son, and Holy Spirit—and our oneness with Them through grace. How amazing is this? The same love the Trinity has for one another is in us who believe (John 17). Grace has become our passion. We believers, like Abraham, are truly the spiritual sons and daughters of God by faith alone (Gal. 3:7–9; Rom. 4:16).

Law vs. Grace

Law...	**Grace...**
Demands righteousness *Rom. 8:3,4; Col. 2:13,14*	Gives righteousness *Rom. 5:17; 2. Cor. 5:21*
Produces sin *Rom. 7:8–11; 5:20*	Provides righteousness *Rom. 5:19-21*
Requires love *Matt. 22:35–40*	Offers love *1 Cor. 13; Gal. 5:6*
Frustrates *Acts 15:10,11*	Satisfies *Matt. 11:28–30*
Condemns *Rom. 5:16,18; 2 Cor. 3:9*	Justifies *Rom. 3:24; 5:18*
Makes guilty *Rom. 3:19; Jas. 2:10*	Sets free *Rom. 8:2; 6:22; Gal. 4:4–7*
Subjugates *Col. 2:20–23; Rom. 8:15*	Reigns *Rom. 5:20,21*
Weakens *Rom. 8:3; Gal. 4:9*	Empowers *Acts 4:33; 2 Cor. 12:9*
Kills *2 Cor. 3:6,7; Rom. 7:9*	Gives Life *John 10:10; Rom. 6:11–13*

Old Testament law and New Testament grace cannot coexist, because they belong to different economies with different goals in mind. As I have already stated, grace confirms that the law is good, and Calvary love fulfills its Old Testament revelation on how to treat God, self, and others. Therefore, the law and grace are contrary to one another. The one was a temporary addition, and the other a permanent fulfillment of the promises.

The following New Testament scriptures will help you settle once for all that Moses' law, though good, holds no legal power over us in this Dispensation of Grace: "whatever the law says, it says to those who are under the law" (Rom. 3:19); "by the deeds of the law no flesh will be justified" (Rom. 3:20); "now the righteousness of God apart from the law is revealed" (Rom. 3:21); "the law brings about wrath" (Rom. 4:15); "sin is not imputed when there is no law" (Rom. 5:13); "the law entered that the offense might abound" (Rom. 5:20); "the law has dominion over a man as long as he lives" (Rom. 7:1); "if her husband dies, she is free from that law" (Rom. 7:3); "you also have become dead to the law through the body of Christ" (Rom. 7:4); "the sinful passions which were aroused by the law" (Rom. 7:5); "now we have been delivered from the law" (Rom. 7:6); "I would not have known sin except through the law" (Rom. 7:7); "For apart from the law sin was dead" (Rom. 7:8); "I was alive once without the law" (Rom. 7:9); "what the law could not do in that it was weak through the flesh, God did by sending His own Son" (Rom. 8:3); "Israel, pursuing the law of righteousness, has not attained to the law of righteousness" (Rom. 9:31); "Christ is the end of the law for righteousness" (Rom. 10:4); "the strength of sin is the law" (1 Cor. 15:56); "for by the works of the law no flesh shall be justified" (Gal. 2:16); "as many as are of the works of the law are under the curse" (Gal. 3:10); "no one is justified by the law" (Gal. 3:11); "Christ has redeemed us from the curse of the law" (Gal. 3:13); "if the inheritance is of the law, it is no longer of promise" (Gal. 3:18); "the law…was added…till the Seed should come" (Gal. 3:19); "if there had been a law given which could have given life, truly righteousness would have been by the law" (Gal. 3:21); "we were kept under guard by the law, kept for the faith which would afterward be revealed" (Gal. 3:23); "the law was our tutor to bring us to Christ" (Gal. 3:24); "But after faith has come we are no longer under a tutor" (Gal. 3:25); "the heir, as long as he is a child…is under guardians and stewards until the time appointed by the father" (Gal. 4:1,2); "we were children…in bondage.… But when the fullness of time had come, God sent forth His Son…to redeem those who were under the law, that we might receive the adoption as sons" (Gal. 4:3–5); "because you are sons, God has sent forth the Spirit of His Son into your hearts, crying out, 'Abba, Father!'" (Gal. 4:6); "Therefore you are no longer a slave but a son, and if a son, then an heir of God through Christ" (Gal. 4:7); "You have become estranged from Christ, you who attempt to be justified by law" (Gal. 5:4); "if you are led by the Spirit, you are not under the law" (Gal. 5:18); "having abolished in His flesh the enmity, that is, the law of commandments" (Eph. 2:15); "not having my own righteousness, which is from the law, but that which is through faith in Christ" (Phil. 3:9); "the law made nothing perfect" (Heb. 7:19); "the law, having a shadow of the good things to come, and not the very image of the things" (Heb. 10:1); "whoever shall keep the whole law, and yet stumble in one point, he is guilty of all" (Jas. 2:10).

The New Creation Case Against the Legal Power of the Law over Us Today

1. **The law revives sin and brings death.**
   I was alive once without the law, but when the commandment came, sin revived and I died.

   Rom. 7:9
   (also 7:8–11)

2. **The law cannot justify.**
   Therefore by the deeds of the law no flesh will be justified in His sight, for by the law is the knowledge of sin.

   Rom. 3:20
   (also Gal. 2:16; 3:21; Heb. 7:19)

3. **The law was a shadow.**
   For the law, having a shadow of the good things to come, and not the very image of the things, can never with these same sacrifices, which they offer continually year by year, make those who approach perfect.

   Heb. 10:1

4. **Christ is the end of the law.**
   For Christ is the end of the law for righteousness to everyone who believes.

   Rom. 10:4

5. **We receive righteousness without the law.**
   But now the righteousness of God apart from the law is revealed, being witnessed by the Law and the Prophets,

   Rom. 3:21

6. **We are saved by grace through faith, not the law.**
   For by grace you have been saved through faith, and that not of yourselves; it is the gift of God,
   not of works, lest anyone should boast.

   Eph. 2:8,9

7. **We are dead to the law.**
   Therefore, my brethren, you also have become dead to the law through the body of Christ, that you may be married to another—to Him who was raised from the dead, that we should bear fruit to God.

   Rom. 7:4
   (also Gal. 2:19; Rom. 7:8)

8. **We are redeemed from the curse of the law.**
   Christ has redeemed us from the curse of the law, having become a curse for us (for it is written, "*Cursed is everyone who hangs on a tree*"),

   Gal. 3:13

9. We received the Holy Spirit by faith, not the law.

O foolish Galatians! Who has bewitched you that you should not obey the truth, before whose eyes Jesus Christ was clearly portrayed among you as crucified?

This only I want to learn from you: Did you receive the Spirit by the works of the law, or by the hearing of faith?

Are you so foolish? Having begun in the Spirit, are you now being made perfect by the flesh?

Have you suffered so many things in vain—if indeed it was in vain?

Therefore He who supplies the Spirit to you and works miracles among you, does He do it by the works of the law, or by the hearing of faith?—

just as Abraham *"believed God, and it was accounted to him for righteousness."*

Therefore know that only those who are of faith are sons of Abraham.

And the Scripture, foreseeing that God would justify the Gentiles by faith, preached the gospel to Abraham beforehand, saying, *"In you all the nations shall be blessed."*

So then those who are of faith are blessed with believing Abraham.

Gal. 3:1–9

10. The law is good, and there was a time when it was the only standard of righteousness to live by; nevertheless, today in this Dispensation of Grace Christ is our righteousness, and God's love is the standard by which we measure our godliness.

For the commandments, *"You shall not commit adultery," "You shall not murder," "You shall not steal," "You shall not bear false witness," "You shall not covet,"* and if there is any other commandment, are all summed up in this saying, namely, *"You shall love your neighbor as yourself."*
Love does no harm to a neighbor; therefore love is the fulfillment of the law.

Rom. 13:9,10
(Gal. 5:6)

On the cross of Calvary, the love that has always existed between the Father, the Son, and the Holy Spirit emerged from the shadows, types, and promises of the Old Testament into rich fulfillment. "In other words," states Manson, "Jesus not only brings the revelation of God, *He is the revelation.*"[2] At last we could see a Man who was the express image of the Father, lovingly ministering grace and truth to everyone by the Spirit, laying down His life for all sin on the cross and taking it up again three days later, giving us all hope forever.

Love and Grace

God's love gave us grace, and grace sets us free to live by His love. There is no other way that fallen man could rise up and consistently live by the kind of love that belongs to God alone. Only grace enables us to do so and look good all the time. It is the key to our consistency. It never changes; we may, but it never does. It is our constant helper. It is always there for us. Grace is ours today, tomorrow, and forever because of Christ's righteousness and not our own. Grace makes life good all the time. It always gives us a happy ending. Shout "grace, grace" and live by love, and look like God all the time, thanks to Jesus and His righteousness (Rom. 5:17,21).

Thus it would be by grace alone through faith that man could be reconciled to God and restored to fellowship with Him.

His sacrifice on the cross said, "We want to share the love that has always been Ours with you. We have paid the full price for you to come and join Our eternal fellowship." What greater proof could we have of our loving God than this? "Thus God is never to be thought of as something different from what he has made known about himself in the person of Jesus and revealed to us by the Spirit," declares Coppedge.[3]

The grace of salvation has set us all free to unashamedly walk with God at all times. This freedom it offers is freedom indeed and knows no boundaries. Through grace, believers are no longer "mere men" (1 Cor. 3:3); they are brothers and sisters of Christ and members of God's family. They are spiritual giants. They walk with God. Our conversation needs to be reorientated to reflect a salvation-centered lifestyle, and not, as it is far too often, a sin-centered one. Which do you think brings more glory to God? Which do you think helps man more? Which glorifies Christ and His cross? Grace is our unequivocal answer. Yes, grace has changed everything. Christian, don't ever forget that it is grace alone that makes you look like Jesus. No amount of good works can achieve this. Shout "grace, grace," forget your past, and move on!

Today we live in the Dispensation of Grace (Eph. 3:2). Everything God does is grace-oriented. This is the most unique time to live in before the coming of Christ. This grace has empowered us to freely walk away from (1) the legal right of the law of Moses to condemn us, (2) the old, fleshly bondages that enslaved us, (3) those sins that ensnare us, and (4) the family iniquities that used to overtake us and run our lives. Whatever personal ministry we need to help us along the way should be welcomed by us from our gifted, anointed ministers and professionals in our churches. Let grace reign!

Grace Has Given All Believers a New Creation Identity

It would be Christ's loving revelation of grace and truth that would enable man to be saved and return to love; furthermore, "this action of grace…is intended to bring about a renewed *humanity*, wherein God's purpose for both the individual and the race reaches its fulfillment," writes G. R. Beasley-Murray.[4] This truly is a return to Eden.

At long last grace has birthed a new creation that has returned to love as our best answer, and it buzzes with the anticipation of the quickening in the end when God will be all in all once again and our return to Eden will be complete. At last love will fill everything. "For glorified man," as Kline described it, "earth [will] become 'heavenized.' All [will] be aglow with glory."[5] And Beale adds, what "began in Genesis 2 but was abandoned will be commenced again and completed in Christ and his people, and will encompass the whole new creation."[6]

This is where the healing process of all human relationships begins, for, as Darrell W. Johnson asks, "How can we stand or sit or be within the circle of God's knowing of himself and not learn to love one another?"[7] The lessons learned from Calvary love enable families and their churches to rise up and become shining examples of this dispensation and the glorious, eternal age to come.

Our every blessing in Christ comes to us by grace through faith alone. Let this cut you loose to live by Calvary love without fear. Christian, you are free. It doesn't get any better than this. Boldly return to your God and enjoying, knowing, and experiencing love without the law. Christ's righteousness by grace through faith is enough for God and should be enough for you and me. We are saved by grace, and we also reign in life by grace (Rom. 5:17).

Christian, you are no longer on the run; the devil is. These days, when things go wrong, whether it is your fault or not, don't avoid God and His people and allow yourself to be deluded into feeling secure in your old fleshly "hiding place," as Bonhoeffer described Adam's error in the garden.[8] This is the voice of the enemy. Instead, answer love's call and come running to Him and share your heart with Him because you know He is always seated on a throne of grace and can't wait to embrace you and your problems and counsel you (Heb. 4:14–16). Bring your failures into His light and boldly live by grace, because though you may at times come short, Christ's grace is more than sufficient. Look at your life and see how His grace has always been there taking care of you. Christ's righteousness is yours today, tomorrow, and for the rest of your life regardless of your old flesh. Thank God for grace to reign in life through Christ! Find a church that lives this, and ask God to add you there. Be empowered by grace.

Love birthed the grace and truth that fallen man needed to receive their new creation identity in Christ. Therefore, believers today don't need anything more than Christ to be recognized as children of God. Their new status is a spiritual one in Christ, and that is enough for God and should be enough for you and me. Schweizer wrote, "No law hems us in any longer, not even the law of self-perfection. God loves us before we achieve anything at all.... Because of this we need no longer live in constant fear of appearing inadequate in our own eyes or in the eyes of our fellow men. There is no need to go on searching frantically for our own identity—it has been given to us from the outset."[9] Grace assures us that we look as righteous as Jesus today, and it empowers us to live that way by faith, knowing that in the resurrection we will be like Him in body, soul, and spirit (1 Thess. 5:23; 1 John 3:2; 1 Cor. 15:35–49).

Never forget that to take anything from grace is to ruin it. Add just a little bit of the law to it, and it is no longer grace (Rom. 11:6). In fact, the Scriptures warn us that those who do so fall from grace (Gal. 5:1–9). Grace has high standards of freedom and is very touchy about those who try to qualify them. There will always be those who misunderstand your freedom in Christ—ignore them, run from them, and find some real Christians and enjoy their fellowship.

To attempt to return to the flesh and the law, in part or in whole, is outdated. It is to fall from grace (Gal. 5:4). It is to abandon the love that brought it to us through the cross. In the resurrection grace's work in our lives will be completed and all the promises given Abraham and the prophets will have come to pass through the second Adam, Jesus Christ.

> And so it is written, *"The first man Adam became a living being."* The last Adam became a life-giving spirit.
> However, the spiritual is not first, but the natural, and afterward the spiritual.
> The first man was of the earth, made of dust; the second Man is the Lord from heaven.
> As was the man of dust, so also are those who are made of dust; and as is the heavenly Man, so also are those who are heavenly.
> And as we have borne the image of the man of dust, we shall also bear the image of the heavenly Man.
>
> *1 Cor. 15:45–49*

We are living at a time when the reaping of the great end-time harvest has been initiated, and grace on a scale never seen before is the powerful vehicle God is using to bring it to pass.

Grace has enabled the weak and the strong, the poor and the rich, the guilty and the innocent, the Jew and the Gentile, to be saved. This is how He has always intended to fulfill the promises made to Abraham through Christ about his future sons and daughters who would be as numerous as the stars in the sky and the grains of sand at the seashore. What a privilege to be living in this amazing Dispensation of Grace, which is the precursor to the eternal age to come.

Salvation through Christ by grace is the only way back to Eden's love. What was lost in that garden has been regained by the triumph of the cross of Jesus Christ. He is the One that God had planned from the beginning to be the scapegoat for all sin so that He might be able to offer the way back free of charge at His own expense: "For by grace you have been saved through faith, and that not of yourselves; it is the gift of God, not of works, lest anyone should boast" (Eph. 2:8,9). Salvation by grace alone is the greatest proof we have of God's love, and this is exactly how He planned it to be. It says, "I want you back in My eternal arms of love, regardless of your past or your present problems." Grace is the answer. It is the only way back to Eden's love. Christ has restored our personal relationship to God forever.

Grace says, "It is I alone who makes it possible for you to return to Eden's love and rise in the resurrection in the end with all the saved." The Old Testament law could not do this. It was designed to create the need for grace and point to its many blessings through Christ. Grace takes away man's bragging rights. It gives them all to the cross (Gal. 6:11–14). It humbles sinners and the saved. No wonder Käsemann wrote, even "piety that stands in the way of love stands in the way of God himself, and no theology or dogmatics has the slightest justification for arguing to the contrary."[10]

Christ's righteousness by grace through faith has made it possible for God to justify the worst of sinners: "But where sin abounded, grace abounded much more, so that as sin reigned in death, even so grace might reign through righteousness to eternal life through Jesus Christ our Lord" (Rom. 5:20,21). Paul's grand conclusion was this: "sin shall not have dominion over you, for you are not under law but under grace" (Rom. 6:14).

Today grace is God's answer to everything believers ever face. "Reign in life by grace through Jesus" is His counsel (Rom. 5:17). Too many well-intentioned Christian authors and teachers of no small reputation have misunderstood grace. In their enthusiasm for righteousness they have inadvertently made it an end in itself, thus opening the door to the compromise of its freedom by promoting legalistic living. In many circles they have left those who received the revelation of grace under suspicion and even doubt. This is too bad, because grace is God's best news for needy man; no act of righteous devotion can do more for us than what the cross has already accomplished and grace has freely given. Stand in grace and pursue love by grace, and you will look like God.

Jesus, a New and Living Way

> Therefore, brethren, having boldness to enter the Holiest by the blood of Jesus,
> by a new and living way which He consecrated for us, through the veil, that is, His flesh,
> and having a High Priest over the house of God,
> let us draw near with a true heart in full assurance of faith, having our hearts sprinkled from an evil conscience and our bodies washed with pure water.
> Let us hold fast the confession of our hope without wavering, for He who promised is faithful.
> And let us consider one another in order to stir up love and good works,
> not forsaking the assembling of ourselves together, as is the manner of some, but exhorting one another, and so much the more as you see the Day approaching.
>
> *Heb. 10:19–25*

Much of religion has placed the cart before the horse, and its emphasis is on man's works and not on Christ's finished work on the cross. They have forgotten that Eden was all about fellowship with God, and not working hard to make a friend. Believers are a people at rest, and the lost ever remain in conflict. "Only in Jesus, therefore," noted Thornton, "can man become that significant whole for which he was originally created."[11]

Christ's Grace Changes Everything for God's New Creation *(Rom. 5:20,21)*

> ...But where sin abounded, grace abounded much more,
>
> *Rom. 5:20*

Sin abounded	vs.	Grace abounded much more

> so that as sin reigned in death, even so grace might reign through righteousness to eternal life through Jesus Christ our Lord.
>
> *Rom. 5:21*

Sin reigned in death	vs.	Grace...reigned to eternal life

This is Paul's explanation of how Jesus took care of the sin problem. And what is the only conclusion? In this Dispensation of Grace, sin is no longer the hot issue for believers; grace is. Hear the conclusion of Rom. 5:20,21:

1. The opposite of sin is abounding grace.

2. The opposite of sin's reign of death is grace's reign of eternal life.

This sounds very provocative and leads some to ask, "Are you saying that sinning doesn't matter anymore in this

Dispensation of Grace?" The answer of grace is this: "No, it does not in the same way it did under the law." Back then it condemned you, but today it is simply a reminder of who you were and no longer are. Grace has set us free from the legal condemnation of the law, although the Scriptures certainly teach that sin is contrary to our death, burial, and resurrection with Christ, and it ever remains a potential for bondage, and who needs that (Rom. 6)! However, this concession in Romans 6 must not be allowed to detract from the freedom grace affords every believer. God's new creation specializes in grace, not sin (Rom. 5).

Every time you say the word "grace" you are actually speaking of the outrageous, undeserved, excessive generosity of Christ's righteousness that has justified you, empowered you, set you free from sin forever, and enabled you to reign in life. For God's new creation, the opposite of sin is not "not sinning," but grace. They know that Jesus is their only hope, and while the resolve not to sin looks good from the religious point of view, only walking by faith in Christ's righteousness by grace impresses God: "If we live in the Spirit, let us also walk in the Spirit" (Gal. 5:25).

Of course James, the brother of Jesus, wrote in his epistle, which was penned before Paul's full-blown revelation of the Dispensation of Grace with all of its ramifications, that those who would live by grace ought to walk in the humility of Christ, lest God resist them (Jas. 4:6). Paul came along after that, writing to the church members in Rome on how to walk as new creation, saying, "Put on the Lord Jesus Christ, and make no provision for the flesh, to fulfill its lusts" (Rom. 13:14), without the legal bondage of the law hanging over their heads. He phrased it differently when he gave similar advice to the Ephesian church members, "be imitators of God as dear children" (5:1), giving them a threefold outline on how to do so: (1) "walk in love" (5:2–7); (2) "walk as children of light" (5:8–14); and, (3) "walk circumspectly, not as fools but as wise" (5:15–21ff.).

Grace Sets Believers Free Forever

God is righteous in offering grace to whoever will receive it, because of Jesus who paid for it with His own blood. Grace leaves believers debt-free for life. Yes, grace is so amazing, because while the law weakened man, making his worst points show up (Rom. 7:8–11), Christ's grace strengthens man and makes him look as righteous as Jesus all the time. In fact, grace empowers us to reign in life in those areas where our worst points once brought us so low (Rom. 5:17; 2 Cor 12:9). Sometimes we reign in life over them, and sometimes we reign in life in spite of them, but always with shouts of "grace, grace!" We shout "grace" at our successes. In fact, we shout "grace, grace" at everything. It is our code word for "Jesus," and it says, "Because of His righteousness I can, and I will. To God alone be all the glory!" Watch me go to the top, not because of myself, but because of Him and His righteousness by grace.

Grace is often misunderstood because of how freely it will help anyone. As I have stated, grace will gladly rescue the good and the bad, the strong and the weak, the right and the wrong, etc. Grace doesn't have a conscience. Grace doesn't take sides, because it doesn't care who was right and who was wrong. Christ's righteousness has prequalified everyone who has turned to Christ and believed unto salvation. Grace justifies. Therefore, it is like a blind lover who believes everybody is beautiful because all it knows is the cross. It comes straight from God's heart of love to help you in your time of need (Heb. 4:16) and asks for nothing in return, only that you turn to Christ and His cross and believe.

In Christ, believers have been restored to fellowship with God because they are as righteous as He—justified forever. Now they are ready to return to Eden's love.

Grace Is Your Enabler

(Here is a sampling to consider.)

1. **To Save You**

   …by grace you have been saved through faith,…

   Eph. 2:8–10

2. **To Stand In**

   …this grace in which we stand,…

   Rom. 5:1,2

3. **To Build You Up**

   …His grace, which is able to build you up…

   Acts 20:32

4. **To Reign in Life**

   …receive abundance of grace…

   Rom. 5:17,21

5. **To Prosper You**

   …the grace of God bestowed…

   2 Cor. 8:1,6,9

6. **To Empower You**

   …"My grace is sufficient for you,…"

   2 Cor. 12:9

7. **To Gift You**

   …we have received grace…

   Rom. 1:5

8. **To Help You to Serve**

   …grace, by which we may serve God…

   Heb. 12:28

9. **To Experience His Love in Church**

   …this grace was given,…fellowship…

   Eph. 3:8–21

10. To Justify You Always

...justified freely by His grace...

Rom. 3:24; Titus 3:7

It is because of grace that our righteousness looks like Christ and not us, and it is about time we gloried in that and stopped trying to do so in each other's flesh. This shortsightedness has given the unbelieving world the wrong impression of Christians and left them ignorant of the grace that empowers believers to reign in life by faith alone; therefore, they look for glory in man, and not in Christ where it should be found. It has made Christianity about man's performance, and not Christ's on their behalf. It has put the emphasis in the wrong place—man, and not God. In fact, it has created a whole new paradigm around man and his works. It has made Christianity humanistic rather than theistic. As a result we point to man instead of Christ to see a good Christian.

What we need in Christianity is a new spirit of loving grace, a new reputation for the unconditional acceptance of the needy because of Christ and His sacrifice alone. Jesus needs to become the only one in the spotlight. Once again society should ring with the glorious message of Jesus and His righteous atonement for all sin and the grace He extends to everyone to be loved and accepted, warts and all. Christians owe it all to Him. Grace will change your life and win you over to God and true godliness. It will also make you very grateful and release you to walk with God in true righteousness by faith with a sweet spirit.

Grace Makes Everyone a Winner

Grace takes away everyone's excuse for failure through the limitations of the flesh. It empowers. In Christ's kingdom there are no losers or victims—all are victors in Christ. Grace has opened wide the door for every believer to be more than a conqueror through Jesus Christ regardless of their flesh. It strengthens them so that they can do all things through Christ. Grace makes you a miracle-worker. There is no end to what you can do through grace right now. It means that anyone, even the weakest among us, can do anything and become anything by grace.

> But by the grace of God I am what I am, and His grace toward me was not in vain; but I labored more abundantly than they all, yet not I, but the grace of God which was with me.
>
> *1 Cor. 15:10*

Jesus has pleased the Father for us. Our victory cry is "Grace, grace!" and not "Look at me!" The flesh must ever remain a nonentity compared to our joy in the Lord by grace. We are a people at rest in our Savior and not our flesh (Heb. 4:1–11). Christians must brag on Jesus and stop bragging on one another. Flattery is an awful thing; it robs Jesus of His glory.

Do You Know What Is in You?

> that the sharing of your faith may become effective by the acknowledgment of every good thing which is in you in Christ Jesus.
>
> *Philem. 6*

The acknowledging of every good thing in you is not a goal—it is a declaration of faith in what God has done in you.

And what good thing is in you? The answer is Christ through the Holy Spirit and all the promises of a restored relationship. This is already there in you. It is yours. This is the gift of grace and not your works.

> that the name of our Lord Jesus Christ may be glorified in you, and you in Him, according to the grace of our God and the Lord Jesus Christ.
>
> *2 Thess. 1:12*

Every good thing in Christ is in you right now, waiting to be acknowledged and taken advantage of.

This is the new you, and it wants to be recognized and released. Only you can set the new you on the inside free to live the superabundant life Jesus died to give you.

It is yours. It is in you. It is the real you since the moment you were saved.

Acknowledge* it and enjoy your new life!

The greatest problem Christ's new creation faces is not lack, but ignorance of what is in them through grace.

Stop acknowledging the "old man" and identifying with it and ignoring who you have become in Christ, a new man. Christian, this is the real, eternal you.

The old = the old ways in your flesh.

The new = the new ways in Christ.

Acknowledge What Is in You

1. Newness—a new heart

> "I will give you a new heart and put a new spirit within you; I will take the heart of stone out of your flesh and give you a heart of flesh."
>
> *Ezek. 36:26*

* Gk. *epignōsis*—recognition; full discernment; acknowledgement.

2. Wholeness—you are complete in Him

and you are complete in Him, who is the head of all principality and power.

Col. 2:10

3. Oneness—unity of the Spirit

I, therefore, the prisoner of the Lord, beseech you to walk worthy of the calling with which you were called,
with all lowliness and gentleness, with longsuffering, bearing with one another in love,
endeavoring to keep the unity of the Spirit in the bond of peace.
There is one body and one Spirit, just as you were called in one hope of your calling;
one Lord, one faith, one baptism;
one God and Father of all, who is above all, and through all, and in you all.

Eph. 4:1–6

4. Fullness—a new song, voice, submission

And do not be drunk with wine, in which is dissipation; but be filled with the Spirit,
speaking to one another in psalms and hymns and spiritual songs, singing and making melody in your heart to the Lord,

giving thanks always for all things to God the Father in the name of our Lord Jesus Christ,
submitting to one another in the fear of God.

Eph. 5:18–21

5. Love—rooted and grounded

that Christ may dwell in your hearts through faith; that you, being rooted and grounded in love,
may be able to comprehend with all the saints what is the width and length and depth and height—
to know the love of Christ which passes knowledge; that you may be filled with all the fullness of God.

Eph. 3:17–19

6. Greatness—greater is He who is in you

You are of God, little children, and have overcome them, because He who is in you is greater than he who is in the world.

1 John 4:4

7. Boldness—power, love, and a sound mind

Therefore I remind you to stir up the gift of God which is in you through the laying on of my hands.
For God has not given us a spirit of fear, but of power and of love and of a sound mind....

> For this reason I also suffer these things; nevertheless I am not ashamed, for I know whom I have believed and am persuaded that He is able to keep what I have committed to Him until that Day.
>
> *2 Tim. 1:6,7,12*

8. Optimism—the hope of glory

> Now may the God of hope fill you with all joy and peace in believing, that you may abound in hope by the power of the Holy Spirit.
>
> *Rom. 15:13*

We are no longer striving to look like Christ, because our new man already does, and we are learning to walk in this newness every day by faith: "But we all, with unveiled face, beholding as in a mirror the glory of the Lord, are being transformed into the same image from glory to glory, just as by the Spirit of the Lord" (2 Cor. 3:18). He is our "mirror image" (Col. 3:9,10). This mirror image is who you are in Christ, and it is also your prophetic destiny. It is your spiritual right today to celebrate your newness. This is why our boasting is in Jesus and His cross, and not us. Nothing can beat what He has done in us. We now live by love, standing in His grace, following in His footsteps by faith. We have traded in our self-assurance for "Christ-assurance."

The Holy Spirit Is Our Teacher

In this dispensation there is a new Teacher and guide from heaven—the Holy Spirit of truth (1 John 2:20,27; John 16:13). He is also the One who leads us personally in our churches, comforting us with the promises (John 16:7–15). As Martyn Lloyd-Jones stated, "Christians are who they are because of the Holy Spirit."[12] He is our Friend on Jesus' behalf.

It is God's plan that those who are born again receive the firstfruits of His Spirit as a gift and seal on their lives (Rom. 8:23; 2 Cor. 1:22), empowering them to live miraculously. This is God's perfect gift to the saved (2 Tim. 1:6,7; Acts 2:38; 11:16,17). It is also proof positive that they belong to God and will one day be gathered together in Him in the Father in the end after the resurrection (Eph. 1:9–14). The Spirit is "the seal of God's people, the badge of their sonship, and the earnest of their future inheritance," agrees Newbigin.[13] The gift of the Holy Spirit is the source of the blessings promised to Abraham's sons and daughters of faith. It is the messianic sign that He now reigns, and the beginning of the new is upon us before the end. He is the gift of grace.

...an epistle of Christ...by the Spirit (2 Cor. 3:3)
(Rom. 2:12–29; 2 Cor. 3:1–18)

The Gentiles	**The Jews**	**The New Creation**
Rom. 2:12–16	*Rom. 2:17,18*	*Rom. 2:28,29*
By nature	By the law	By the Holy Spirit
...the work of the law written in their hearts,	...rest on the law, and make your boast in God,	...circumcision is that of the heart,
...their conscience also bearing witness,	and know His will,	in the Spirit,
...their thoughts accusing or else excusing them...	and approve the things that are excellent, being instructed out of the law,	not in the letter; whose praise is not from men but from God.

...of the Spirit... (2 Cor. 3:6b)
...transformed...by the Spirit... (2 Cor. 3:17,18)

Christ's new creation is of another Spirit. This dispensation of grace has made it possible for Christ's new creation to be full of the Holy Spirit—led, taught, guided, and inspired by Him—a testimony of newness from the inside out. A dancing, skipping, jumping, laughing, eternally free people prosperous in every way—the envy of the whole world. A people of righteousness, peace, and joy in the Holy Spirit. This is Christianity at its best, and anything else is a lesser experience. The "life-giving spirit," Jesus in your heart—could you expect anything less? Could you want anything more? Receive Him, be set free by Him, and live the superabundant life He came to give you. Christian, He is your true power source.

Truly the life source of God's new creation is the Holy Spirit. He is the One who turns believers into epistles of Christ by writing the story of God's love through the cross, first in their heads and then in their hearts (Heb. 8:10). This is something the law wasn't designed to do. Paul said that the words carved in stone were life-killers, but the words carved in our hearts by the Holy Spirit are life-givers (2 Cor. 3:1–6). This is grace at its best.

Instead of being guided by the law written in stone the way they were under Moses in order to be good covenant-keeping Jews, today under the New Covenant we are spiritual Jews guided by grace and led by the Holy Spirit as He writes in our hearts, teaching us how to live by love according to the New Covenant promises, free from condemnation (Rom. 8:1). Stand on the promises and shout "grace, grace!"

From Revelation to Revolution

The accuser's blame game has been nipped in the bud. He has been thrown out of heaven along with his bad attitude, and it is up to us to stop listening to his lies and replace them with the assurance we have in Christ's righteousness by grace. We are blessed. Renew your mind with the promises of God and stand boldly. This may sound too good to be true, but it is not. Your healing is dependent on this. You are free at last to walk with God and make Him your best and dearest Friend.

Grace has freed believers from living with condemnation and weakness forever (Rom. 8:1). We never go any further back in our thoughts than Romans 5:1—we live justified lives, and this is as good and, yes, as bad as it will ever get. Reign in life through Christ's righteousness by grace and live well. Thank God for the power, love, and sound mind that is now yours through the Holy Spirit's anointing (2 Tim. 1:7). Stir this up, not your old flesh.

Changing our religious mindset to think grace thoughts is fundamental to learning to walk in the newness that is ours in Christ. Therefore, the Scriptures speak of being "transformed by the renewing of your mind" (Rom. 12:2), and they admonish us to "no longer walk as the rest of the Gentiles walk, in the futility of their mind" (Eph. 4:17), and again to "put off…the old man [the lost person you were]… and be renewed in the spirit of your mind, and that you put on the new man which was created according to God" (Eph. 4:20–24). Bad theology leads to bad thinking and bad speaking and bad living. We are Spirit-led, and not fearfully driven by the law. Our days of striving are over—since we were saved, it is revelation that empowers us to grow by grace. The more you learn about Jesus from the Holy Spirit, the more you will see Him as your mirror image.

Grace has taught us how to live full of hope in this world, in spite of its negativity, with the assurance that we are not a part of it anymore. Settle this: you have been delivered from it. You don't belong. As N. T. Wright puts it, you are part of "the renewed human race,...the new type of humanity."[14] Your eyes have been opened, and now you can see through its ruse. Jesus has overcome the world for us (John 16:33), and through grace we can once again take dominion over it, bringing it into subjection to the knowledge of Christ (2 Cor. 10:4,5).

The pleasures of life that God has given us on this earth to freely enjoy have been given back their shine. We are not religious nuts who, as Dick Westley wrote, "have been overfed a theology of sin."[15] We live superabundant lives (John 10:10). We enjoy great relationships. We, like our Creator God, are extravagant and live life to the full, but not to the same excess as the world which mistakenly tries to find purpose and fulfillment in pleasure (1 Pet. 4:1–4). Our pleasure is born of contentment in Christ, Who is our

Lord and Savior and elder Brother. We have learned to enjoy our human experience prior to the resurrection in the end (1 Cor. 15:22–24) through our fellowship with God. We live well, we are content, and we enjoy the difference. We live by a new paradigm. We are the envy of the world. We have it made coming and going. My prayer for you is the same as John's: "Beloved, I pray that you may prosper in all things and be in health, just as your soul prospers" (3 John 2).

Thanks to grace, the pressure has been taken off us to get things right all the time; we "can take the risk of failure," Schweizer wrote.[16] Because of grace, our lives are no longer sin-centered, but salvation-centered, and we love it. God sees us through Christ and not our flesh, and we see ourselves the same way. This is true love. Christian, you look good. Thank God for amazing grace!

CHAPTER 5

Experiencing God's Love

Real Christians Love like Jesus

Jesus came to reveal God in person. In fact, He revealed Him to be Three Persons—Father, Son, and Holy Spirit—and yet one God. And what makes Them one? Love! Yes, They are all perfect in this one thing: They are full of a love that is unique to Them alone. In this perfection They are holy. Yes, this love is the source of Their glory, and from it came all life and light and everything They made.

Love is who They are, what They are like, and how They do everything They do, because "God who is love naturally acts toward the world in accordance with the eternal divine essence, which is love," declares Grenz.[1] It helps to put in perspective false religion's abuse of words such as *righteousness*, *holiness*, *sanctification*, etc., because they need to be seen as reflections of God's love and not legalistic, religious terms we frown on in this so-called post-Christian era. They reflect the behavior of love, which takes the edge off their potential for legalistic living in this Dispensation of Grace. Thank God for saving grace and imputed righteousness.

Theirs is a very unique relationship, and They chose to make man and invite him to share in this amazing love They enjoy, to the awe of the angelic host. This was "a fruit of God's longing for 'his Other' and for that Other's free response to the divine love," wrote Moltmann.[2] The Triune God's creative act arose, Torrance adds, "out of that movement of sublime Love within himself, and its free movement outward from himself toward us in his will…to share the fullness of his Love in fellowship with others…."[3] "God's own character can only be mirrored by humans who love after the manner of the perfect love which lies at the heart of the Triune God," wrote Grenz.[4] Thus man was made for relationships by the One who wrote the book on relationships.

Through the Cross Love Has Opened the Door to Unending Fellowship with God

> "I do not pray for these alone, but also for those who will believe in Me through their word;
> that they all may be one, as You, Father, are in Me, and I in You; that they also may be one in Us, that the world may believe that You sent Me.
> And the glory which You gave Me I have given them, that they may be one just as We are one:

> I in them, and You in Me; that they may be made perfect in one, and that the world may know that You have sent Me, and have loved them as You have loved Me."
>
> *John 17:20-23*

The miracle of God's new creation is that they have been invited to share in the love that exists between the Father, Son, and Holy Spirit (John 17:23b), Who are the eternal "social Trinity, the community of love," Grenz tells us.[5] It is this grand experience of love between believers and their God that they have brought into their homes and churches and every area of their lives. It sets them apart from the rest of the world as a one-of-a-kind people (John 17:21). Their relationships smack of Eden's bliss. They are full of the joys of togetherness, the pleasures of companionship, and the excitement of unending, inseparable love between them, their God, and everything they ever do. This is true prosperity. This is their glory. This is God's glory!

This is the perfection that God calls His new creation to live by (John 17:23a; Rom. 13:8; 1 John 4:12)—"loving even those who have least claim or right to our love," writes Walter Wink.[6] This is the glory of God that should be manifested in our lives (John 17:22,23) and our churches (Eph. 3:21). This is man's destiny: show off Who God is and what He has done for us all. Ernst Lohmeyer noted for us, "The variety and multiplicity of commandments fade away or are comprehended in the simple commandment concerning love. This simplicity is at the same time the eschatological seal of God's House and Kingdom. Likewise and for the same reason the Gospel demands of men what is virtually impossible: 'You must be perfect, as your heavenly Father is perfect' [Matt. 5:48] and demands it…as the one thing possible and necessary.…So there takes place, as if it was the most natural thing on earth, that miracle which blends holiest law and man's heart of hearts in purity: love God and love your neighbour…."[7]

Jesus exalted love "above every other principle governing duty," wrote Manson, "a love like that of God Himself, extending even to sinners and enemies."[8] His teachings are all love-based, and they are all we need to know to please the Father. As real and significant as the knowledge of good and evil might be, it is subordinate to the way, the truth, and the life found in Jesus Christ. His love alone must define them. "This love and grace," wrote Anton Fridrichsen, "are now the principle of life, the power and the rule of those who have been made righteous."[9]

Read again Jesus' language to His Father about us in John 17: "I…pray for…those who will believe in Me (v. 20)…that they all may be one, as You, Father, are in Me, and I in You; that they also may be one in Us (v. 21),…And the glory which You gave Me I have given them, that they may be one just as We are one (v. 22): I in them, and You in Me;…You…have loved them as You have loved Me (v. 23). Father, I desire that they also whom You gave Me may be with Me where I am, that they may behold My glory which

You have given Me; for You loved Me before the foundation of the world (v. 24). O righteous Father! The world has not known You, but I have known You; and these have known that You sent Me (v. 25). And I have declared to them Your name, and will declare it, that the love with which You loved Me may be in them, and I in them" (v. 26).

You are everything to God, and His Son's willing death on the cross proves it; in fact, wrote Dick Westley, "Jesus… *is* the revelation that it is the Father's fondest desire to enter into a relationship of intimacy with each of us."[10] Actually, this prayer reveals beyond a shadow of a doubt that believers are in a completely different class than the rest of humanity and that they are destined to be part of God's family in the most intimate fashion. "And Jesus tells us that it is for that intimacy we were created and redeemed," states Johnson. He adds, "We are all wired for intimacy.…[A]ll our thirsts are ultimately thirsts for the passionate belongingness of God."[11] We were made for love and to live by God's love alone.

It is worth noting that twice in this prayer to His Father, Jesus says of this great love relationship we have with them and one another in our homes and churches, "That the world may believe" (v. 21), and again, "That the world may know" (v. 23). God's love is our brand, and its mark on our lives is our trademark. Of this scripture, Paul Minear wrote, "God's name is love. In manifesting God's love through his ministry and death, Jesus revealed that name.

The work of making that name known will continue to the ends of the earth and the end of time. Wherever God's love fills the ministry of Christ's people, there Christ himself is at work. The love of God incarnate in Christ and embodied in Christ's community—this love is the way God has chosen to make his name known to all men."[12]

Regarding Jesus' prayer, Johnson wrote, "At the center of the universe is intimacy, a deep, abiding, tender, affectionate belonging. The Father really loves the Son. And the Son *really* loves the Father. And that love, that intimacy, is so real it is embodied in the Holy Spirit."[13] And now because of Jesus this loving intimacy includes us and is in us.

After reading John 17:20–26, who cannot help but believe, and who can keep themselves from loving God with all their heart? Thank God, getting saved has qualified you to do so. I know I cannot resist Him! And what is the conclusion? Father, Son, and Holy Spirit are Three in One, and since the cross that number includes you and me in that fellowship as His sons and daughters forever.

Man has only been able to say "us" about their oneness with Christ since they were saved. Never before has such a thing been true. Not even Adam and Eve could say "us." The best they could say was that God walked in the garden and visited with them, but never "us" as we do today. This was grace's greatest work.

Today as Christ's new creation, believers can boldly say "us" about being in Christ and their oneness with Him. In fact, they can never be anything less than "us," and they don't need to be anything more. "Us" is enough. Nothing is more satisfying than this "usness" we have with God. It almost sounds blasphemous to the uninformed hearer, too good to be true.

I often say "us" to myself over and over again—us, us, us, us, us—and then I laugh and say, "Thank you, God!" In my most intimate moments with Him I whisper "us" with great fondness and deep gratitude. He always smiles and says "us" back to me.

Thank you, Jesus, for "us." I will never get over it, and I don't think anyone who knows this will either. Jesus has restored our relationship to God and enabled us to join Their family of love. No wonder the unity of believers is so important to God; it is a reflection of the power of love that makes us one when it is at work in our homes, churches, and anywhere else believers are found. Unity is the fondest reflection of the love that exists between God the Father, the Son, and the Holy Spirit that we can experience in this lifetime.

A Word to the Overzealous: Love Is to Be Our Governing Principle, Not Moses' Law

The Scriptures call love "the greatest commandment," "the first commandment," (Matt. 22:37–40; Mark 12:29–31) and "the new commandment" (John 13:34), depending on which dispensation you are living in.

The whole purpose of the Old Testament was summed up by Jesus in one word, "love" (Matt. 22:36-40). He said that all the books of the law and all the books of the prophets in the Old Testament "hang on" love alone (v. 40). All He left out were the history books and the poetry and wisdom books when He said this. In other words, in spite of all the legalism, love was also the prevailing revelation in the Old Testament. Too many have missed this.

The New Testament continues the same theme. Love sent Jesus to earth, He lived by love, and love sent Him to the cross. His message was about love, and He commanded His followers to live by love, "the highest of the absolutes of Jesus," as Manson wrote.[14] John, in his epistles, went so far as to say that to live by love was proof positive that we are disciples of Jesus. Schweizer wrote, "the all-embracing gift of the Spirit is love";[15] and of the three greatest gifts (1 Cor. 13:13), it alone "abides into eternity," writes Fee.[16]

False religion has lost sight of this. It has added many things to love that are not necessary, and it has taken religion way beyond relationships to something else—vain opinions and rituals. One result is that "religion makes it harder for us to believe that God really loves us, that he forgives us, that he wants us to be truly free in his presence so we can be living signs of that presence to our world," wrote Dick Westley.[17]

Allow me to be a little forward by suggesting that if a church isn't full of love, it is not a church at all; it is an intimidating, religious gymnasium full of show-offs pumping iron and comparing their muscles. And who wants to be a part of that? Furthermore, if grace, yes, Christ's righteousness by grace alone, isn't the basis for that love, then there is no telling to what lengths you will have to go to live up to everyone's standard of religious correctness, and woe betide you if you fail to do so. No one has ever been able to tally the roll of casualties incurred where love and grace are in short supply and the tree of the knowledge of good and evil is in full bloom, lacing every table with its bounty. Loveless churches are not what Jesus prayed for in John 17.

False religion, this beyond-love religion, is full of condemnation of self and others. Stay away from it! It is self-destructive. It has created a false meter stick by which to measure and control. This has birthed insecurity, weakness, and a diminishing spirit wherever it is preached. It is full of ungrace and is completely without peace, contentment, and especially trust. It makes its followers doubters. They doubt God, they doubt themselves, they doubt one another, and weakness prevails, leading to criticism and judgmentalism on a grand scale. This also turns them into religious show-offs, and who needs that? More often than not it substitutes emotionalism for spirituality. Faith only works by love (Gal. 5:6).

Westley adds, "Religion makes us very untrusting. We don't trust our fellow human beings, we don't trust our God who has revealed that he is at work in all of us, and we ultimately don't trust ourselves either. That makes us fearful, and our fear causes us to revert to force. When we do that, we proclaim to all the world that we don't really know God…."[18]

C. S. Lewis sums it all up this way: "To love at all is to be vulnerable. Love anything, and your heart will certainly be wrung and possibly be broken. If you want to make sure of keeping it intact, you must give your heart to no one, not even to an animal. Wrap it carefully round with hobbies and little luxuries; avoid all entanglements; lock it up safe in the casket or coffin of your selfishness. But in that casket—safe, dark, motionless, airless—it will change. It will not be broken; it will become unbreakable, impenetrable, irredeemable. The alternative to tragedy, or at least to the risk of tragedy, is damnation. The only place outside Heaven where you can be perfectly safe from all the dangers and perturbations of love is Hell."[19]

In contrast, as Christians our conclusions should always be tempered by love and satisfied at times with committing things to God and His better judgment. Let grace reign. Condemnation, criticism, and judgment belong in the kingdom of darkness, not in the kingdom of light. We are not driven by fear. We don't have to get everything right all the time. We don't have to have all the answers today. We are content to walk with God and wait on His good timing. Love trusts. This is the message of abounding grace.

Love is the greatest force in the universe, and it is never going to go away. The God of love will yet inherit all things and fill them with His love. Don't doubt its power for a moment.

Jesus, the Forerunner of a New Humanity that Would Live by Love

As the second Adam, Jesus showed us what the first Adam was like before he fell, and, as Schweizer wrote, in Him "there became visible every moment of God's love which was already at work in creation."[20] As the second Adam, He also achieved "in his person through the Spirit, what the first Adam failed to do," wrote Colin E. Gunton.[21] He, as the "Heavenly Man, the divine prototype of humanity" (Cullmann),[22] accomplished "the latter-day defeat of Satan that Adam should have accomplished in the first garden" (Beale).[23] He won humanity back and restored even more than what was available in the garden—His righteousness by grace to stand in forevermore.

Jesus did not give in to satan's temptation, and revealed the extent of God's love for us when He died on the cross for our sins and overcame the world, the flesh, and the devil for us all. "All that is essential in the work of Christ is summed up in his death on the Cross," wrote Maurice Goguel;[24] thus Calvary love shows us how far God was willing to go to restore us to fellowship with Him. It has released believers to live and love freely again the way it was in Eden. Calvary love has repaired the damage done by satan's reign of fear over man. "Jesus illustrates what people made in the image of God are supposed to be like, and his teaching spells this out," states Coppedge.[25] He never fell short of living by love—which Gordon D. Fee calls "the most essential reality about his character and the absolute predicate of our existence."[26] The plan of salvation has never changed from the beginning. In fact, Thornton wrote, "The whole design of creation was Christ-centred from the first."[27]

"The victory of Christ was won through [His] suffering, self-giving love" on our behalf, as Allison A. Trites pointed out.[28] And He chose this in the freedom of "his vulnerable love, his openness, the encountering kindness through which he suffers with the human beings he loves and becomes their advocate, thereby throwing open their future to them," as Moltmann revealed.[29] The cross was all about crimson love—not ours, but His. Our salvation is the story of grace and "its extension to men in personal relationship," wrote George S. Hendry.[30]

With Christ's death on the cross for all sin and His bodily resurrection from the dead we have the first concrete evidence of how the plan of salvation will end in victory. It is based on a win-win situation—a second Adam who didn't fall prey to satan's deception, and a second or new creation born from His spiritual loins to stand in His righteousness by grace and live by love—"a new lineage, a new people of God," writes Sandra L. Richter.[31] And beyond even that, when Christ rose from the dead with that glorious body that could walk through walls and yet could sit down and enjoy a nice piece of fish, He was showing off the prototype of a new creation of God-birthed people who would one day populate a new heaven and a new earth that was just like Eden, without the tempter's presence. "Christ now is what redeemed man will be," wrote Murray J. Harris. "The glorified Christ is the firstfruits of perfected humanity."[32]

In fact, the new earth would be better than the old one, as Herman Ridderbos stated, wholly in "subjection…to God's perfect dominion."[33] It will be a perfect place full of perfect people, and it will last forever, full of His love. In fact, His resurrection guarantees this.

Our Return to Intimacy

From the beginning of recorded history, man has been trying to better himself and find lasting satisfaction. I suggest that much of this is so because he was made in the image of God for love and is empty without an assured loving relationship with Him. Our best creativity comes from His love, and it is most gratifying; when it doesn't, it is full of man's sinful flesh and is disappointing. Thus, man's destiny is not to vainly chase after everything that comes into his mind but rather to know God and love Him and live in wondrous communion with Him and His people, pursuing life together.

There has been a hole in everyone's heart ever since God was maneuvered out of our lives in the garden, and unfortunately some vainly try to fill it with everything else. Who knows what doors this lack has opened into our souls for the enemy to take advantage of our frustration? Psychologists and Christian ministers alike have had much to say about trying to satisfy these needs. In the words of Peter Kreeft, "Our souls are God-shaped vacuums....This discontent with known earthly joy, this longing for an unknown joy more than earth can ever offer, is the most moving thing in our lives because it is really our longing and love for God, whether we know it or not."[34] Man was incurably hurt at the fall, and only the divine Physician can possibly bring lasting healing to him. This is where the narrative about our return to the Garden of Eden comes into play and finds its legitimacy. It is fellowship with God first, and then fellowship in our homes and churches, by the power of the Spirit, that alone empowers us to live positive, powerful lives full of love. This is our true source of holiness. Churches need a fresh revelation of their important role in man's wholeness.

Many stodgy theologians enjoy telling us that we were made for God's good pleasure. If that was the whole story, He would appear to be selfish and even cold and manipulative; unfortunately, many believe this. The truth be told, God is love, and we were made by the overflow of that love to be loved and to love Him and others in return. Fee wrote, "God's love for us has been 'poured out,' as a lavish and experienced reality, by the presence of the Holy Spirit, whom God has also lavishly poured out into our hearts."[35] In the words of Johnson, "The God who is love draws near to *me*...to draw *me* near to himself, in order to draw *me* within the circle of Lover, Beloved and Love itself. I become a co-lover with God!"[36] This ever remains our destiny to be one with God (love) forever.

This puts a new premium on the revelation of love in the Holy Scriptures and their record of Christ and His disciples. The Bible is our love manual. Markus Barth expressed this by writing, "To listen to the Bible means to listen to the call, the jealousy, the intensity of God's love, and also to hear the manifold reply which God receives from man....The unique power of the Bible flows from the fact that the biblical words are words of love between God and man—a love that comes from God as his free gift; that is repudiated, betrayed, and forsaken by man; and that is nonetheless invincible and succeeds in making men respond with love to God. 'God's love has been poured into our hearts through the Holy Spirit' (Rom 5:5). The Bible is the good news of this love. The reading of the Bible, therefore, should be compared to the reading of love letters, rather than to the study and use of a law book.... The Bible is an invitation to learn of God's love, to enjoy it, and to respond to it."[37]

The mistake Adam and Eve made was to make love selfish, "a perversion of the relation of one human being to another," as Bonhoeffer wrote,[38] and in so doing they became self-consumed and hungry for more than God's love. It was a fleshly kind of love that could not be satisfied in this lifetime. Our unregenerate flesh is insatiable. Thus wickedness was born in the first family. We believers, having received the love of God into our hearts, must be careful not to compromise something so beautiful. God's love is enough all by itself. Feast on it! Such love is the bond of perfection (Col. 3:14). It is the fruit of the Spirit.

We need true intimacy with others of like faith. In fact, God's love makes no sense when you are selfish about it and keep it to yourself, for "love cannot be consummated by a solitary object," Moltmann explained;[39] in fact, "in isolation love dies," wrote John Ortberg.[40] Albertus Pieters informs us that "the New Testament knows of no such thing as a

Christian living in isolation from other Christians."[41] And Grenz adds, "The idea of a self-sufficient, isolated Christian was inconceivable to Christ's first-century disciples. In their understanding, the individual believer and the community were intertwined."[42] James Bannerman stated emphatically, "A solitary Christian is worse than a contradiction, he is an anomaly, standing out against the express institution of God, which has appointed the fellowship of believers in one Church, and made provision in its outward ordinances for their union and edification."[43] Furthermore, Fridrichsen points out, "The New Testament is an ecclesiastical book, and anyone using it to form and foster a private religion for himself abuses his Bible."[44]

Living by love, though very personal, is never a private pursuit or a "mere private, individual experience. On the contrary, the fellowship God intends for us is a shared experience," Grenz writes.[45] "To embrace the gospel, then," wrote Robert Banks, "is to enter into community."[46] Furthermore, adds Bannerman, "The spiritual fellowship that a believer enjoys with his Redeemer, is not a solitary or a selfish joy, but one which he cannot possess alone, or except in common with other believers. It is the very nature, therefore, of the Gospel to be not a solitary religion, but a social one."[47] As I have already stated, it is all about relationships—with God, your family and church, and then in the world as a testimony of the power of the love you are enjoying with your Heavenly Father, His Son the Lord Jesus Christ, and the Holy Spirit.

All of our relationships need to be an extension of what we are enjoying with God the Father's love, the Lord Jesus Christ's grace and truth, and the Holy Spirit's communion (2 Cor. 13:14). In these we know God personally and can recognize the earmarks of our friendship with Him over time. It is a real shame that so many Christians are known for brandishing the truth instead of falling in love with it and loving those for whom Christ died with it. Loving the truth is about loving like Jesus.

At no point can we ever afford to forget that we were made for relationships, that "to be a human being is to be created in and for relationship with God and with other human beings," as Gunton confirms.[48] God's love always belongs to fellowship. It isn't a private feeling; it is more than that. Isolated, it becomes something else—very selfish, which is unlove and not God's love at all. We are called to live by love, and to do so you have to relate to others who are full of the same love. Andrew Jukes pointed out that "to dwell in solitude is not love." More broadly, he said, "If God is love, and love requires such a communion and relationship as is expressed in 'the Name of the Father, the Son, and the Holy Ghost,' then our true life, if we are His sons, must have the same characteristics, and be a life of communion and relationship."[49]

[49] Taken from *The Names of God* Copyright © 1967 by Andrew Jukes, p. 177. Published by Kregel Publications, Grand Rapids, MI. Used by permission of the publisher. All rights reserved.

It is in our churches, those Eden-like communities of love, that God's true intentions for humanity are best shown off. Nowhere else on earth can this be better displayed. They are temples of love, fitly framed by the Holy Spirit for God to once again fellowship with man. Grace has lifted them above the fray, and the voice of the accuser cannot be heard there. The language of love prevails. It is in them that heaven touches the earth again, and God can pronounce His new creation "good" the way He did once before so long ago.

Is God's love important today? Should living by love be important to Christians? The answer is a resounding yes! Love is what we are all about, and in Christ, loving is what we do best. It is the Christian's calling, and it says, "God loves you, and so do I. Come and see and hear for yourself what His fellowship has done for us in our families and churches and what it can do for you as well." We were made by God to live loving lives. It is through God's love that we are destined to conquer the old world and see a new one set up. Unlike false religion, force and violence are not the churches' answer. Love is.

Church Life Is Where Our Love Life with God and Our Divine Connections Are Honed and Enjoyed

Apart from Jesus "there is no saving knowledge of God," writes Coppedge.[50] There is no other way for humanity to begin the return to Eden and the world of love they lived in than this, because Christ, as both the Beginning and the End, "embodies the restoration which he is now effecting in us," Thornton reminds us.[51] Experiencing true love, God's love, begins here. It is only from this place that the Holy Spirit is able to "pour out the love of God in our hearts" (Rom. 5:1–5) and we can start working it into our lifestyles. This is why His followers are called disciples—they copied His lifestyle. Isn't this why they were also called Christians (Acts 11:26)? The hurting world's cruelty is a far cry from Christ's Kingdom of love manifest in His churches.

We will live by love as Jesus and His disciples taught us. It is our chief motive (Col. 3:17; 2 Cor. 5:14). Paul had this to say about living in this present world, yet not being a part of it: "be subject to the governing authorities," to "resist will bring judgment" from them, and to "render therefore to all their due" (Rom. 13:1–7). He went on to say that the only thing that God's people owe is "to love one another" (v. 8) and that "love does no harm" (v. 10). He concludes this chapter by saying, "walk properly" (v. 13), "put on the Lord Jesus Christ [love], and make no provision for the flesh, to fulfill its lusts" (v. 14), which is unlove. By all means, we make the best citizens of any country, and our influence for good is incomparable. Nevertheless, this world is not our home; we belong to a heavenly country. Church life should make the world jealous. It should turn this world upside down.

> "A new commandment I give to you, that you love one another; as I have loved you, that you also love one another.
> By this all will know that you are My disciples, if you have love for one another."
>
> *John 13:34,35*

Love is what Jesus called the new commandment based on the old commandment. The old commandment under Moses' law was to "love the Lord thy God" on pain of death. The new commandment to love is based on God's love for us and our new, soft hearts of love empowered by the Holy Spirit. It is not a command from Moses; it is an invitation from Christ.

Loving flows from our communion with the Spirit of love and our fellowship with believers in our churches. It doesn't seem like a commandment at all when you compare it to the binding law of Moses. Since grace "makes an end of legal religion," as Manson stated,[52] it is more an invitation to stand in Christ's righteousness by grace and let the Holy Spirit live His life of love through us and bear His fruit (Gal. 5:22,23) in spite of our flesh. When this is true in our churches, we won't be able to keep people away. They will be seeking us out. Church life will be the good life.

We are called to enjoy loving freely, because we are freely loved with an unfailing love, an "unending Love that transcends all space and time and all human thought processes in the infinite dimensions of its divine fullness," as Torrance wrote.[53] Moses' administration of the law produced bondage and great fear. Christ's administration of grace sets us free and produces the superabundant life Jesus promised, full of love. In the words of Ernst Käsemann, Jesus broke "through the spell cast by the Mosaic law and the scribes' tradition over the will of God,...to lead men out into freedom."[54] Back then it was "If you fear Me, obey Me." Today it is "If you know My love, live by its overflow from a heart of gratitude" (1 John 3:16,17; 4:7,8). This reminds God of Eden. Grace has taken the pressure off us to get everything right every time, and placed it on the cross.

Thus His new creation fills their toolbox of abilities with the learned experiences they have gained from fellowship with God and other believers. This takes time and practice and includes how we handle the bad times as well as the good, all seen through the eyes of love as we stand in grace by faith, pursuing the Holy Spirit of God. Thus the power of Calvary love becomes ours also. The churches of Jesus Christ should be famous for their loving relationships. How we treat others says volumes about our walk with God.

Christ's Churches Are Centers of Love

There is an inseparable link between living by the love of God in our church relationships and in our homes and then elsewhere. Having been saved since 1965, I am convinced you cannot develop these lessons anywhere better than in these loving places. This is how God always planned them to be. Howard A. Snyder agrees: "There are spiritual truths I will never grasp and Christian standards I will never attain except as I share in community with other believers—and this is God's plan."[55]

Churches teach families how to enjoy one another and receive the most out of home life through their fellowship with God, and their families empower them to grow up to be winners all around. And Erroll Hulse adds, "The light, protection, counsel and loving care which unite in a believing household joined to a believing church constitute advantages and privileges which can never be equalled in any other place, family or environment."[56] They are centers of true prosperity in every sense of the word.

It is there that "the presence of loving relationships between the members provides the most conducive environment within which fuller understanding of God—itself further outworking in love—can be gained," wrote Robert Banks.[57] They are showplaces for the power of God's love. As Peter Leithart stated, "The church is a community dominated, in a word, by *love*."[58]

Christian, God wants His loving relationship with you to affect all your relationships (John 17:26) and to be so real and shocking that you become undeniable proof you are a friend of God. As Jesus said of believers, "that you love one another; as I have loved you.... By this all will know that you are My disciples" (John 13:34,35). Make no mistake about it, our love says we know Jesus and are in fellowship with God. There is not a more spiritual test of our walk with God than this. "This relational capacity is of fundamental importance to our existence, not least because it is the channel through which we express the love of God in our lives," Bray reminds us.[59] After all, the Christian message is "God's multicolored love story," as Kreeft calls it.[60]

It is of value to note that enjoying intimacy with others is not a gift. It is a learned ability. Having the Holy Spirit, Who is full of love, inside you doesn't mean that you automatically know everything about loving. Intimacy with God and others takes a whole lot of faith, time, and practice. Thank God for reigning grace (Rom. 5:17). This is true of all your relationships. As Westley indicates, "The relationship between God and ourselves...is an invitation to loving encounter, intimacy, love, communion, and oneness."[61]

The Christian's honest conclusion is this: the most important thing in life is to experience God's love and then to share it with others. The rewards of doing so are beyond measure, and they make life more beautiful every day as we learn to draw from this.

This is where Christ's new creation churches shine best. God's loving fellowship should be our compass, and the more we allow this to be so, the sweeter things will be. As

James Bryan Smith said, "At the core of our being is a need to love and be loved by others....God has designed us this way because God values human community."[62] This is the way it was with Adam and Eve before the fall, and it is how God's new creation should live today. Our "first calling is truly to be the redeemed community," stated Snyder, "...a microcosm of that cosmic reconciliation [God] is bringing."[63] We bring our fellowship with God (love) into everything. It shapes our new world. It sets us up for eternity.

By experiencing God's love we know Him, and to be without it is to not know Him at all, because God is love (1 John 4:8,16). Receiving this is now on us and not Him. He has done everything to make His love available to us all through the cross. Yet, "Off in the distance God stands alone, with a heart broken because we fail to accept his offer of forgiveness," wrote Smith. "He loves us with a furious passion."[64] And as the father in the parable of the Prodigal Son, "God is looking into the distance for me, trying to find me, and longing to bring me home," wrote Nouwen.[65]

This relationship of love with Him is the reason why Christians cannot have the same intimate relationship with those who haven't been born of the Spirit and experienced His love. No matter how sincere unbelievers may be or how much you may love them, until the love of God comes into their hearts and they learn to live by it, they won't have the same capacity for love as you. Everyone involved will get hurt. True intimacy belongs to God and His spiritual family. Certainly, live by Calvary love, but don't make the mistake of presuming that everyone is ready for the level of relationship that you may have risen to in your walk with God.

Before you became a part of God's new creation you may have had very few interpersonal skills. Perhaps you wrote the book on loneliness and think you have no hope for intimacy. Don't despair, there is hope. Jesus died to restore you to a personal relationship with God and to teach you how to become whole again through His love for you. In Jesus, writes Hendry, God in His grace came "to meet with us humanly and deal with us in human terms, in order to establish with us a truly personal relationship and so to determine our existence in the most fundamental way."[66] Because of Jesus' grace and truth, you can live by love once again in spite of your past or, for that matter, what is going on in your life right now. Through Calvary love you can become the person most sought after by those who used to think you had nothing to offer at all.

Intimacy with God has returned. Love now reigns: "Behold what manner of love the Father has bestowed on us, that we should be called children of God! Therefore the world does not know us, because it did not know Him. Beloved, now we are children of God; and it has not yet been revealed what we shall be, but we know that when He is revealed, we shall be like Him, for we shall see Him as He is" (1 John 3:1,2).

Christian, your days of shying away from relationships are over. In the words of John Ortberg, you can "get the courage to stop hiding" when you know that you are loved.[67] It is time for you to come out of the closet of fear and bad memories, because, as Ortberg also states, "whatever is hidden cannot be loved."[68] You may have been a victim of bad relationships, but in Christ you are a powerful victor. Through His grace you can rise above your fears and dysfunctions. God wants to restore you to wholeness through love in your church relationships. Step out by faith and live the love life on purpose. Open up, be free, receive, and grow. You are safe to do so. Bring the love you and God are enjoying together out of the shadows and into every other relationship by faith, and see what happens.

Churches are a miracle of grace. They are communities of love, and not fellowships of self-righteous believers. There the good and the bad, the weak and the strong, the right and the wrong, live together in harmony governed by God's love, because they glory in the risen Jesus and not one another's flesh. Amazing grace is enough!

Experiencing the power of grace in your church is how "the Holy Spirit ministers to us, in large measure, through each other," explains Snyder.[69] Ministry by grace is the key to living by love, and love is the key to living by grace.

Harold S. Bender wrote, "The church is a community of love—love in action, and love truly exists only in action."[70] I am persuaded that this is where practical holiness begins, not with religious activity trying to please God from the knowledge of good and evil, but by standing in grace (Rom. 5:1,2) and living by love as we look to Jesus and are led by the Spirit. Any other way is medieval and belongs to an empty, outdated religious system that flies in the face of the triumph of the cross on our behalf. Let me remind you that most of European religion is an unholy blend of the Old and New Testaments. However, the new creation message is based solely on New Covenant grace. Thank God, as Jesus said, the church grows by revelation and not old, outdated news (Matt. 16:17,18).

Because of grace, at last we can run free like Adam and Eve. In fact, Leithart tells us, believers are "a race of new Adams and Eves, reborn by water and the Spirit in order to fulfill the original mandate of Adam to worship and obey God and to share His rule over creation.... The church is the fulfillment, the coming into fullness, of the Adamic order. In the church, we find the purposes of God for humanity beginning to be fulfilled. She is the continuing creation of a new humanity in the midst of humanity."[71] As Stanley Hauerwas and William H. Willimon portray the church, they are "resident aliens, an adventurous colony in a society of unbelief."[72] Our churches should be centers of grace. "Each Christian congregation," claimed Newbigin, "is the earnest and foretaste, the *arrabon* of the gathering together of all men of every tribe and tongue around the throne of God and of the Lamb."[73] Banks informs us that "each of the various local churches are tangible expressions of the heavenly church, manifestations in time and space of that which is essentially eternal and infinite in character."[74] This is why they are so important to us. It is in them that we have found the answers we looked for all our lives long. They are the pillar and ground of the truth (1 Tim. 3:15). As Thornton wrote, "The torch of truth displaying the glory of God's love is both Christ on the Cross and also the crucified Lord uplifted in the Church. So long as this dispensation lasts Christ embodied in his Church is the only torch of Gospel truth which men have."[75]

Believers are the set-apart ones who have joined His family of Three. He loves us as much as He loves Himself. How valuable is that? Therefore, believers are called saints—"set-apart ones"—more than by any other name in the New Testament (62 times). And what are we set apart for? First of all, because we belong to Him, and then to enjoy our fellowship with God's people in our churches as a testimony of amazing grace. "His desire is for His followers to be brought into such a unity of love with the Father and the Son that the world might believe," claims David Peterson.[76]

This lies at the heart of the plan of salvation for man. Regardless of the dispensation, salvation has always been about responding to God's love and knowing Him in the context of the particular economy in which they were living with the hope of Christ in their hearts. Since the cross, He has brought all the ethnic groups together "so as to create in Himself one new man from the two," a new humanity (Eph. 2:15), or what Yoder also refers to as "a new social reality."[77] This is God's ultimate triumph for man. This alone is the true "Israel of God" (Gal. 6:16), the ones with whom He has always wanted to share Himself, and it includes every believer who has ever lived.

Paul defined this love in simple terms for the Corinthian church members, saying, God's "love suffers long and is kind; love does not envy; love does not parade itself, is not puffed up; does not behave rudely, does not seek its own, is not provoked, thinks no evil; does not rejoice in iniquity, but rejoices in the truth; bears all things, believes all things, hopes all things, endures all things. Love never fails" (1 Cor. 13:4–8a). "Such love," Fee states, "is the direct result of being loved by the God whose love has been lavished on us in the Son, who likewise loved us and gave himself for us, and by whose indwelling presence we now live."[78] This love eclipses the Law Covenant believers' careful obedience to the Ten Commandments in scope and depth. At best they fall short.

CHAPTER 6

A Perfect Conscience Full of Love

Back to Eden Today

Adam and Eve's sin in the Garden of Eden violated God's love. They chose not to trust Him, and this disobedience changed them from the inside out. Their consciences became unreliable because love was no longer at their core; good and evil were. God did not turn away from man that day; man turned away from God.

Estrangement ensued, which was something they had never experienced before. Friendship with God was lost, and they became afraid. They were also spiritually darkened. The knowledge of good and evil they gained that day added conflict and confusion to their fears. This exposed them to something God would rather they had never found out about. Before they did so, it was the devil's problem and not theirs; however, they made it theirs when they chose to believe his lie, rebel against God, and eat. Don't ever underestimate the negative power of disobeying God. The mistake of choosing to eat the forbidden fruit brought their relationship with God to ruin. Their spirits became dead in trespasses and sins (Eph. 2:1).

At this juncture it might help to be reminded that the tree produced both kinds of fruit—good and evil—and not one or the other. By definition they can't exist without each other. They are ever in conflict, as are those who live by them. Feelings of inadequacy always ensue. Fear always reigns.

The most important question we can ask about Adam and Eve's exposure to the tree of the knowledge of good and evil and its ongoing effect on us all is this: Who profited most from the knowledge they gained and passed on to the rest of humanity? Did God gain anything by their folly? Certainly not. In fact, He warned them not to eat of it. This shows you how much value He put in man's knowing good and evil.

Did man benefit from this knowledge? Did it make him any better? Was the wisdom they gained advantageous to them or their relationship to God? The answer to this is found in the Genesis record—knowing good and evil filled them with fear, drove them from the presence of God, and caused them to hide from Him. As a result, man "no longer regards the other person with love," wrote Bonhoeffer about that event. "The limit is no longer grace that holds the human being in the unity of creaturely, free love; instead the limit is now the mark of dividedness."[1] God never designed man to live with the conflicting knowledge of good and evil. We can't handle it. He made us for Himself, and He is love.

To whose advantage was it then that they ate the forbidden fruit? Man couldn't handle it, and God didn't need them to know of it to better their relationship to Him. The only one who gained the advantage from it was the devil, who is also known as satan, which literally means "accuser" in the Old Testament (e.g., Job 1:6,7). He started the conflict, and he introduced its confusion to man. Thus man's conscience was polluted.

Man's inability to handle the knowledge of good and evil set him up to be accused day and night by satan (Rev. 12:10) and to readily accuse others. It made true religion look bad. It also made man's conscience vulnerable to fear and torment because he didn't know how to live up to this newfound knowledge of good and evil. For example, much like David said of his accusers, "Fierce witnesses rise up; they ask me things that I do not know. They reward me evil for good, to the sorrow of my soul" (Psa. 35:11,12). This sums up the human dilemma.

Accusation is arguably the most powerful tool in satan's hands, and he is the master of it. Through accusation he pits us against ourselves, one another, and even God, and when we fall for that ploy, it is because we have been eating of "the Tree of the Knowledge of Good and Evil and thus do not love," Boyd tells us.[2] We become know-it-alls at the expense of our peace of mind and everyone else's. We don't look like Christ. We no longer trust.

As long as we listen to satan and the voices that accuse us and others in our heads and hearts all day long, our inability to cope with knowing good and evil will continue to make us vulnerable to this trap. Good and evil must be submitted to Calvary love by Christ's new creation, or their consciences will ever remain in fearful torment and full of prejudice. After all, isn't it the minister's goal for us to have the person of Christ formed in us (Gal. 4:19), and not good and evil?

Missing this has given satan power to reshape people, turn families against one another, split churches, and raise generation after generation of people at odds with one another. With the knowledge of good and evil, we are, as the saying goes, "armed and dangerous," and as I quoted Tournier earlier, "there is no one who does not suffer, more or less secretly, from being in conflict with others and from being an agent of division rather than of harmony among men, even though he is quite certain of being in the right."[3] Our only hope is to be liberated by the revelation of God's love and a new way of living by grace alone.

Failure to do so is one of the reasons eastern religions have gained in popularity. People want peace; they want love and not a fight. Many are willing to try anything to find relief from the never-ending feelings of guilt and regret produced by accusation. What good is a religion that provokes conflict rather than peace of mind? Christianity is in retreat wherever they preach that tree. Christ's victory on our behalf is complete; enjoy!

An Upgraded Conscience

As Christians, there is no other way to stop the madness the tree produced than to upgrade our consciences to reflect this dispensation's new creation message of grace and love. John Ortberg explains, "Spirituality rightly understood is life. It is the humble reception of grace and the confident embrace of love. Spirituality wrongly understood is death: a major source of human misery and rebellion against God."[4] David Peterson adds, "[W]hen we overwhelm people with conditions which they must fulfil to prove that they are making progress as Christians, we distort the gospel."[5]

The reality is, guilt, shame, criticism, judgmentalism, and condemnation will continue to tear us apart until we are saved and allow Christ's love to rule in our hearts and minds by grace. Embracing Christ and His kingdom of love is our only answer. Jesus came to restore man's broken fellowship with God and return him to a conscience full of grace and truth guided by love. This is another reason why church life is so important—it is a fellowship of love. It is there that we experience Calvary love in action as grace reigns.

A New Creation Conscience Based on New Building Blocks

God's new creation people are in a class all by themselves. They have a unique worldview because, as Hauerwas and Willimon state, they are "the only community formed around the truth, which is Jesus Christ, who is the way, the truth, and the life,"[6] and there has never been anyone like them on this planet before. "The love inspired by Christ was an absolutely new thing in the religious history of man," proclaims Manson.[7] They have a new conscience based on a new rule—the cross (Gal. 6:14–16). This has given them a new, peaceful, inner guide. Their consciences are free—no more madness. They see life through the cross.

What God wants from us today is a lifestyle of love that emulates Christ, and as Ortberg reminds us, the Scriptures and modern science tell us that "love and fear are literally incompatible in our bodies."[8] Furthermore, as we settle this, let us never forget that our love doesn't come from us, but rather from His love for us and in us. Our love is responsive. "God's love for us generates our love for God, for ourselves, and for all others," wrote Boyd.[9] And Thornton explained that "the loving response of the Son to the Father is the sphere in which the response of our love is born."[10]

Christ's churches are "outpost[s] of the heavenly city," as Thornton and others describe them,[11] in a world of accusation, crying out for relief from the torment of the forbidden knowledge. In church the love of God should be on display as its members "manifest the integrity and purity of a life moved by the love of God," Peterson wrote,[12] and the flesh with its many negative voices has been brought into subjection to the knowledge of Christ (2 Cor. 10:4,5). Love has won; grace abounds. The unlove of the world would fill us with confusion, but God's love has filled His new creation and their churches with the light of the glorious Gospel of Christ's righteousness by grace (Rom. 5).

As Eduard Schweizer points out, "In Jesus therefore a whole new world has come into being. Different laws are now in effect."[13] Yes, indeed, grace reigns. This is what we build our consciences on in this Dispensation of Grace. The question then is, practically speaking, how do we go about doing this?

The Five Building Blocks of a Christian Conscience in This Dispensation of Grace

1. My sin debt has been paid off.

= I am forgiven.

(A blood-sprinkled conscience)

Jesus didn't just die for this sin or that; He died for all sin, and that included every sin that had been committed or would be committed to the end. His sacrifice was complete, and it was the last sacrifice God would ever require for sin. In Him our forgiveness is complete and final. Christ has dealt with the sin issue permanently on the cross.

> For such a High Priest was fitting for us, who is holy, harmless, undefiled, separate from sinners, and has become higher than the heavens;
> who does not need daily, as those high priests, to offer up sacrifices, first for His own sins and then for the people's, for this He did once for all when He offered up Himself.
>
> *Hebrews 7:26,27*

His once-for-all sacrifice has given believers a once-for-all forgiveness and a standing in His righteousness by grace forevermore. This is the basis for what the writer of Hebrews calls the better promises (Heb. 8:6).

We are forgiven forever by grace through faith in Christ the day we are saved. And though you are not perfect in practice, and life may try to hold you accountable for your actions, in Christ, God won't do so. Jesus is on your side. Never forget that today He is our Advocate (1 John 2:1), not our adversary.

Thank God for churches that believe and practice this. They are lighthouses of hope in a dark world tormented by guilt. We are destined by God to show off the power of the cross to forgive, and not the power of our flesh to condemn and never forget.

You have been forgiven and declared as righteous as Jesus because of the sacrifice He made on your behalf. Here on out He deals with you and me as sons and daughters, not as condemned sinners. We are family now. We are His new creation in Christ. Sin is no longer the hot issue; living by love and so satisfying the royal law is (Jas. 2:8). Christian, you have been completely forgiven, and nothing can separate you from the "inalienable love of God" through Jesus Christ, as Manson put it.[14] Because you have embraced this love, He will always work things together for your good. This is what God's amazing grace is all about. As a child of God, nothing, not even your failures, can sever you from His love.

Christians have been forgiven, and every sin issue they ever have to deal with thereafter must be from the vantage point of justification and not condemnation. In the words of H. R. Mackintosh, all legalistic thought has been put "out of court in a religion of unreserved grace."[15] Settle this once and for all: God is for you, and He will never be against you ever again (Rom. 8). In 1645 Samuel Bolton declared, "Christ Himself shall as soon be called to account for your sin as you yourself. If you have an interest in Him, sin shall never condemn you, for Christ has made satisfaction for it."[16] Believers have been born again to live free again the way it was in Eden.

Christian, be bold to stand in who you are in Christ, forgiven, cleansed, and justified, with a blood-sprinkled conscience. The sin issue died with Christ, so "reckon yourselves to be dead indeed to sin, but alive to God in Christ Jesus our Lord" (Rom. 6:11). Remember, "he who has died [with Christ] has been freed from sin" (6:7). Why? Must I repeat the legal case for our freedom in Christ? For those doubters, I will: Sin can only take dominion over a man by the power the law gives to it, and Paul confidently declares that "sin shall not have dominion over you, for you are not under law but under grace" (6:14). Therefore, those days of doubting whether your sins have been forgiven are over. Not only has your sin debt been paid off, but you are no longer under the law, but under grace. Full atonement has been made, and you are forgiven forever. Live like it. There is nothing left to condemn you. How exhilarating!

2. My bondage to dead works is over.

= I am free.

(A purged conscience)

The second building block builds on the first. *I am forgiven*; therefore, *I am free* "from dead works to serve the living God" by the Spirit alone (Heb. 9:14). Not only are we forgiven through the sprinkling of His blood, but this has brought the Law Covenant works system to an end.

There is nothing left for us to do, and we don't have to wear ourselves out trying to impress God or gain His favor through religious dead works anymore. As Mackintosh reiterates, "Justification is exclusively God's work; man cannot contribute to it but only put hindrances in the way."[17] There is nothing like the freedom of coming to rest in Christ's works, knowing He has already pleased God on our behalf, and not being works-driven to try to please Him ourselves. On this basis His "approach to us is made in freedom and is reciprocated in freedom," wrote Hendry.[18]

A new freedom now rules our relationship with Him, and nothing can change this. What we do for Him today is of the Spirit from a heart of loving gratitude. As Erroll Hulse wrote, "Good works are our daily concern. Yet these works are always performed out of love and gratitude, never out of servile fear or through the false idea that we can earn God's favour by them."[19] Ours are works of praise and thanksgiving, not for merit, because there are no "have-to's." We never have to earn God's love. Francis Schaeffer stated, "We say 'Thank you' for work completed upon the cross, which is sufficient for a completely restored relationship."[20] To attempt to work to please God or maintain your salvation, whether in part or whole, is to fall from grace (Gal. 5:4). Jesus fulfilled all the works of the law for us.

The day of metaphors has passed and along with it the works that were a "shadow of the good things to come" (Heb. 10:1). We are now living in the Dispensation of Grace, which Abraham Booth called a "covenant of absolute promises with no conditions to be fulfilled."[21] Thank God, the real has arrived, and we now live accordingly. Jesus Christ has fulfilled all the shadows and types for us and become the Mediator of a new and better covenant (Heb. 8:5,6). We are free. We are at rest. The gift of salvation is ours, and we have been made acceptable in the Beloved (Eph. 1:6). As R. C. Sproul reminds us, the "perfect active obedience of Christ fulfills all righteousness, earning all the merit needed to save the believer. Nothing can be added to Christ's atonement or to his righteousness to enhance their value and merit."[22]

The writer of the Hebrew epistle reminded those church members of the "perfection of Christ's self-offering as the sacrifice to end all sacrifices," and the "power of his blood to effect purification at the level of the conscience, to liberate people from the guilt associated with 'dead works', and to set them free to serve God in a new way," Peterson wrote.[23] As surely as they had passed from death to life in Christ, so also should their consciences be updated to reflect, not a dead legalistic system—what E. F. Scott referred to as "the long reign of mechanical legalism"[24]—but a new and living way made possible through Jesus Christ by grace alone. Having been made free indeed, they should now live free lives, looking forward to their eternal inheritance with boldness (Heb. 9:9–15; 10:19–23). Shouts of "grace, grace" are in order! God has already made us accepted in the Beloved (Eph. 1:3–6). This is a lifelong promise.

He is in love with you. By all means love Him back because you want to and not because you are still trying to impress Him. Through the cross He has won you to Himself. Enjoy the loving relationship. There are no more conditions to satisfy.

Paul's legal conclusion to the Galatian church members was, "Stand fast therefore in the liberty by which Christ has made us free, and do not be entangled again with a yoke of bondage" (Gal. 5:1). The rigid requirements of false religion are that bondage, and those days of hard work are over—the eternal age of Abrahamic blessing by faith alone has dawned. We are free. He said to those believers, "So then those who are of faith are blessed with believing Abraham" (Gal. 3:9).

Any works we now perform in service for God are by the Spirit and His easy leadership in our lives based on a heart of gratitude full of love. "The very act of ministering the truth to one another should be an exercise of love," declares Peterson.[25] We are led by the Spirit and no longer driven by our insecurities.

We now serve "the living God" (2 Cor. 3:3) through our partnership with the Holy Spirit, and the good works we perform together are of a completely different genre—love. Now what we do is the faith-based fruit of our love relationship with Him, full of gratitude and not expediency. It is part of our sacrifice of praise and thanksgiving.

Accordingly, our bondage to dead works is over—we are free!

3. My relationship to God is now based on who I am in Christ alone.

= I am standing in grace.
(A secure conscience)

The third building block builds on the first two. *I am forgiven, I am free,* and now *I am standing in grace.*

This is the key to Christian victory: standing in Christ's righteousness by grace. There is no other way to reign in life than this (Rom. 5:17–21). And, as Manson wrote, "being in Christ means having Christ not merely as the ground, or as the sphere of our new Christian life, but as its substance."[26]

The believer's righteousness is a given righteousness. It is a free gift by grace through faith alone (Rom. 5). It is Christ's righteousness that has been imputed to us (1 Cor. 1:30; Rom. 4:23–25; 2 Cor. 5:21). Paul's prayer was, "that I may gain Christ and be found in Him, not having my own righteousness,...but that which is through faith in Christ, the righteousness which is from God by faith" (Phil. 3:8,9).

> But when the kindness and the love of God our Savior toward man appeared,
> not by works of righteousness which we have done, but according to His mercy He saved us, through the washing of regeneration and renewing of the Holy Spirit,
> whom He poured out on us abundantly through Jesus Christ our Savior,
> that having been justified by His grace we should become heirs according to the hope of eternal life.
>
> *Titus 3:4–7*

The best thing you will ever do for yourself is to start enjoying the righteousness that grace guarantees everyone who is in Christ. We live by grace, not our righteousness.

In the sight of God our personal righteousness is as "filthy rags" (Isa. 64:6), and all that impresses Him is our standing in Christ's righteousness by grace alone. This knowledge saved me in 1965. I know I now look like Christ to Him, and I have learned to see myself that way too. Truly grace is amazing.

Until your conscience reflects Jesus' victory on your behalf, you will always be reflecting the weakness of your flesh, not the power of reigning grace. This may drive you "away from God into [your] secure hiding place," wrote Bonhoeffer, where you will be living by your "own good and evil,"[27] constantly making your victory flimsy and uncertain. No one will ever go much further than their conscience will allow them; it is not only our guide, but also a thermometer reflecting our soundness. Right believing produces right living. Christian, you must start believing that your righteous standing in Christ through grace is all you will ever need to be what God wants you to be and to do what He has planned for you to do. Look to His righteousness by grace for confidence, not to your old fleshly man.

Faith in His Son is the only way to please God in this Dispensation of Grace. Access the free grace based on Him alone, and run with God with shouts of "grace, grace" in spite of your problems. Learn to overcome by the Spirit of grace and not be intimidated by your humanity. Getting saved is about Jesus, not you. Get over the lie. Fellowship with believers who live this way, and be built up in the power of the grace life. As I have already stated, Christ's righteousness by grace makes you look good all the time.

Your conscience must always protect and insist on your legal right to stand in grace and "reign in life" (Rom. 5:17–21). This is the new creation miracle mind-set. Shut your flesh up and, for that matter, everybody else's, and enjoy grace. Never again must believers look to self for their confidence. There must be a thought change, a speech change, and a life change to match up with grace. Banish terms such as "self-confidence," "self-assurance," etc., and replace them with confidence and assurance in Christ by grace alone. The miracle of the new creation is Jesus, not self. Under the law, believers were called to be personally strong; however, under grace we are called to "be strong in the Lord and in the power of His might" (Eph. 6:10).

Therefore, those weak in the flesh can be strong in the Spirit, the poor rich, and the small can do great things through grace. At last we are as righteous as God Himself because of Christ our righteousness, and His "perfect sacrifice…provides the basis for relating to God under the new covenant," Peterson asserts.[28] Remember, you stand in His righteousness by grace alone.

4. My Christian service is now based on Calvary love.

= I am empowered to live by Calvary love.
(A pure conscience)

The fourth building block builds on the first three. *I am forgiven, I am free, I am standing in grace,* and *I am empowered to live by Calvary love.*

Getting saved is about restoring our relationship to God so that we can live a loving life, free from condemnation. Through the grace of the Lord Jesus Christ we are empowered by the Spirit to do exactly that, love like Him. This is why we have turned our backs on religious legalism and the condemnation, fear, and torment it produced. Because of grace Christians have a "received love," and they are growing in a "learned love" in their churches, where they are taught to "give away" God's love freely by grace. This is what believers and their churches should look like. They are communities of love that have entered into the oneness of love that exists between God the Father, God the Son, and God the Holy Spirit. This is how God receives glory in the church by Christ Jesus (Eph. 3:21).

Because the Holy Spirit is the Spirit of love and lives in our hearts, everything He does or gets involved in is always love-based (Rom. 5:5). Our "only law [is] the inner law of love written on the heart by the Spirit," as James P. Hanigan wrote.[29] This is another reason why everyone who is a part of God's new creation must reorientate themselves to living by Calvary love and not the baser motivations that drive the world.

None of us can afford to forget for a moment that we are a people of the future living today, showing off the love of God that will fill the new heavens and earth in the end after the resurrection. Today we do so by the grace of God through the power of the Holy Spirit within, looking forward to its fullness. Living any other way falls short of our destiny. Anything less turns the Holy Spirit off (Eph.

4:29,30). As Gordon D. Fee wrote, we are "an eschatological community, whose members live in the present as those stamped with eternity. We live as expatriates on earth; our true citizenship is in heaven (Phil. 3:20)."[30]

Paul wanted them to understand that the love life believers live today is not because of them and the goodness of their own hearts. If this were the case it would soon run dry. The new creation has been empowered by the Holy Spirit to invite Christ into their hearts by faith and live by His love and not theirs.

This is a miracle of grace. Yes, this is where our Christlike love comes from—a revelation of Him and His love for us that we have invited into our hearts and live out by faith looking like Him.

> And we have known and believed the love that God has for us. God is love, and he who abides in love abides in God, and God in him.
> Love has been perfected among us in this: that we may have boldness in the day of judgment; because as He is, so are we in this world.
>
> *1 John 4:16,17*
> *(2 Cor. 2:15,16; Gal. 4:19; Eph. 4:13)*

The glories of Christ's present-day Messianic reign in our hearts motivated Paul's prayers for the Ephesian church members. One of them (Eph. 3:14–21) contains the how-to on being empowered by the Holy Spirit to live by Calvary love with Christ in our hearts: (1) "be strengthened* with might through His Spirit in the inner man, (2) that Christ may dwell* in your hearts through faith; (3) that you, being rooted^ and grounded^ in love, may be able to comprehend* with all the saints [fellow church members] what is the width and length and depth and height—(4) to know* [experience] the love of Christ which passes knowledge [through how you treat one another]; (5) that you may be filled* with all the fullness of God" (Eph. 3:15–19; see note below). Walking in Calvary love makes you a bigger, better person—Christ-like. And Schweizer reminds us that "the gift of the Spirit makes us open to other human beings. For whoever has been liberated from self is also liberated for the one who needs his love."[31]

It is in this same atmosphere of heartfelt love that we are released to develop our spiritual gifts in our churches as we line up our thinking with who we have become in Christ by the Spirit, and love others on His behalf (Rom. 12:1–7). Thus the call of God on our lives continually man-

* All of these verbs (*strengthened, dwell, comprehend, know, filled*) are in the Greek aorist tense—usually a simple past tense, but here as a single occurrence that happens at a point in time. How thrilling to know that these have already happened to us. They are a done deal. We are already strengthened. Christ already dwells in our hearts, etc.

^ These two verbs (*rooted, grounded*) are in the Greek perfect tense—a one-time occurrence with continuing effect. They are always true. They never stop being so. We have been and are always rooted and grounded in Christ's love, etc.

ifests as we find opportunity to lovingly exercise our gifts, which Fee calls the "concrete expressions of the grace of God at work in the life of individuals for the sake of others."[32] Thank God for churches that help their people to develop their gifts as a manifestation of their loving relationship to God.

Our Christian service is truly free—from His heart to yours and back to Him again with love—and everyone else gets in on the benefits. Speaking the truth to one another should be like giving away love (Eph. 4:15,16). Don't ever allow it to go beyond this and become an instrument of condemnation.

Believers have embraced love as their answer and chosen to walk in it by the Spirit, enjoying their pure conscience. Truly we are a people excited about serving the invisible God for no visible reason other than obedient faith working by love (Gal. 5:6), or as Fee adjusts the translation, "faith expressing itself through the Spirit's fruit of love."[33] His love has changed us forever. Before we were saved, we experienced it from afar as we looked at the cross. Now it is inside us through the indwelling Holy Spirit, and we will never be the same. "It is love which we know only through Christ dwelling in our hearts and through the Holy Spirit who sheds abroad the love of God into our hearts," wrote T. F. Torrance[34] (Rom. 5:5). It is also all around us as we recognize God's loving hand at work on our behalf in all things.

Calvary love is the new "wisdom of God," and, empowered by His Holy Spirit of love at work in our churches, we are destined to influence the world for good (Eph. 3:10).

5. My conscience is being transformed by the Word ministry.

= I am abiding in
what the Holy Spirit is teaching me.
(A good conscience)

Abiding in the Word ministry of the Holy Spirit in your church is the last building block. *I am forgiven, I am free, I am standing in grace, I am empowered to live by Calvary love,* and *I am abiding in what the Holy Spirit is teaching me.* This completes the foundation on which to build your new creation conscience.

Paul said we are a "word of faith" people (Rom. 10:8). This is why believers love their Bibles so much. Its teachings are what we base our belief system on.

The Old Testament saints had a veiled understanding of their Scriptures. On the other hand, New Testament saints have a revealed understanding of the Scriptures (2 Cor. 3:12–18) based on Jesus Christ and His message of grace and truth.

Thus believers today live by the teachings of the Lord Jesus Christ and His apostles, which collectively are called the New Testament Scriptures. Spiritually, as Jesus promised, we have a new Teacher Who confirms all truth in our hearts. He is the Holy Spirit (John 16:13). However, in practice we have many teachers through whom He works: ourselves in personal study, our fellow church members, the teaching ministry of our senior minister and his ministerial team, etc.

When it comes to living by the Holy Bible, our consciences draw from two sides of the Holy Spirit's Word ministry:

1. **Our Holy Bible, the written Word of God** (Gk. *logos*, Eng. *word*—the general Word). This is where we learn about the Dispensation of Grace and the new creation message of love by the Spirit, etc.

> and that from childhood you have known the Holy Scriptures, which are able to make you wise for salvation through faith which is in Christ Jesus.
> All Scripture is given by inspiration of God, and is profitable for doctrine, for reproof, for correction, for instruction in righteousness,
> that the man of God may be complete, thoroughly equipped for every good work.
>
> *2 Tim. 3:15–17*

The following verses are a few examples of the word *logos* in the Holy Bible. The English translation of this word is highlighted in the text:

> For the **message** of the cross is foolishness to those who are perishing, but to us who are being saved it is the power of God.
>
> *1 Cor. 1:18*

> In Him you also trusted, after you heard the **word** of truth, the gospel of your salvation; in whom also, having believed, you were sealed with the Holy Spirit of promise,
>
> *Eph. 1:13*

> having been born again, not of corruptible seed but incorruptible, through the **word** of God which lives and abides forever,
>
> *1 Pet. 1:23*

Evangelicals are quick to declare that the Word of God is their sole rule of faith and practice.

2. **Scriptures from our Holy Bible, the Holy Spirit's Word ministry in our hearts** (Gk. *rēma*, Eng. *word*—the applicable Word). This is the word that the Holy Spirit is working into our hearts and has also given us the grace to believe and embrace by faith.

Believers today also build their new consciences on the specific lessons learned from the Holy Spirit's ministry in their hearts. This is why they put such a premium on His anointing in their services and their private times with Him when He is teaching them from the Scriptures. Believers are called to abide in or stick with what the Holy Spirit has taught them.

> But you have an anointing from the Holy One, and you know all things....
> Therefore let that abide in you which you heard from the beginning. If what you heard from the beginning abides in you, you also will abide in the Son and in the Father.
> And this is the promise that He has promised us—eternal life.
> These things I have written to you concerning those who try to deceive you.
> But the anointing which you have received from Him abides in you, and you do not need that anyone teach you; but as the same anointing teaches you concerning all things, and is true, and is not a lie, and just as it has taught you, you will abide in Him.
> And now, little children, abide in Him, that when He appears, we may have confidence and not be ashamed before Him at His coming.
> If you know that He is righteous, you know that everyone who practices righteousness is born of Him.
>
> *1 John 2:20,24–29*

Now here are a few examples that use the word *rēma*, referring to the taught Word or believed Word. The English translation of this word is again highlighted:

> For He whom God has sent speaks the **words** of God, for God does not give the Spirit by measure.
>
> *John 3:34*

> "It is the Spirit who gives life; the flesh profits nothing. The **words** that I speak to you are spirit, and they are life."
>
> *John 6:63*

> So then faith comes by hearing, and hearing by the **word** of God.
>
> *Rom. 10:17*

The New Creation Has Updated Their Consciences to Reflect Their Faith in Christ's Forgiveness, Freedom, Grace, Love, and the Word of God

While the Law Covenant promises were good, today believers live by better promises. They enjoy, therefore, a better hope through Christ that has given them a new creation conscience. At last they can truly say that their consciences are based on a "better covenant" with God. The old Law Covenant has been fulfilled and no longer applies to them as a legal system to live by.

New creation believers build their consciences on better promises.

> for the law made nothing perfect; on the other hand, there is the bringing in of a better hope, through which we draw near to God.
>
> *Heb. 7:19*

> But now He has obtained a more excellent ministry, inasmuch as He is also Mediator of a better covenant, which was established on better promises.
>
> *Heb. 8:6*

It is through the Word ministry that new creation believers grow practically into the image of Christ.

> clearly you are an epistle of Christ, ministered by us, written not with ink but by the Spirit of the living God, not on tablets of stone but on tablets of flesh, that is, of the heart.
>
> *2 Cor. 3:3*

> But we all, with unveiled face, beholding as in a mirror the glory of the Lord, are being transformed into the same image from glory to glory, just as by the Spirit of the Lord.
>
> *2 Cor. 3:18*

These five building blocks of our new creation conscience are the key to fulfilling your prophetic destiny to show off Christ in us and our churches.

New creation believers must, therefore, adjust their thinking to the cosmic change that has taken place since the cross, or they will be out of step with this Dispensation of Grace. Having done this using these five building blocks, they can now rest assured that their inner guide, their consciences, reflect Christ's Gospel of grace instead of the old Law Covenant days, which have been fulfilled by Christ and have "vanished away" (Heb. 8:13; 10:9). In other words, if it is out of God's sight, put it out of yours. Christian, upgrade your views. Your personal relationship to God is now based on the grace of our Lord Jesus Christ alone.

Reigning in Life by Grace with a New Conscience

Rely on your new creation conscience to instruct you. Count on it to guide you. Allow the Holy Spirit to build it up through the Word ministry. Don't be intimidated by false religion or your old flesh, which is no longer you. Edify the new you with new thoughts about you from the better promises of the New Covenant message of grace.

Regardless of what you have to face in the future, whether of your own making or not, don't go back to the tree for your answers (1 Cor. 4:3–5), and don't mix with those who do so. Those days of daily feeding on a diet of fruit salad picked from the tree of the knowledge of good and evil are over. Jesus has made this so. This bad habit needs to be broken. It's up to you to stop looking at life through the first Adam's eyes. The second Adam has a new worldview. Embrace it. Boldly show it off to the world. This is real Christianity.

The devil knows you no longer belong to him—you have been bought with a price by Jesus (1 Cor. 6:20)—and he cannot legally trouble you anymore. However, this doesn't mean to say that he has given up on trying to accuse you anyway. You don't have to listen to his lies and try to justify yourself; you know that Jesus has already taken care of this on the cross. The devil has no power over you. You have found refuge under the Lordship of Jesus Christ in your church—stand strong in Him, because you are safe. Believe God and the better promises of the New Covenant, and not his lies.

I know that Christ's new humanity is made up of the most joyous, life-filled people on the planet, because their consciences have found rest. The confusing knowledge of the tree of good and evil no longer dominates their lives; the love of God does. They think differently; they have the mind of Christ (1 Cor. 2:16). Furthermore, they have been adopted into God's family through Christ. They are no longer the poor, sickly kids on the block, living under the circumstances. They are blessed. They are too busy prospering in everything even as their souls prosper (3 John 2) to waste their time with negative thoughts about themselves or anyone else for that matter. They have been set free by Christ's grace to reign in life (Rom. 5:17), be more than conquerors (Rom. 8:37), triumph always (2 Cor. 2:14), and do all things through Christ Who is their strength (Phil. 4:13).

This kind of right thinking empowers us to live by the new system that Christ has set up, and be a testimony to the failure of the old system, which Yoder called a system of "structured unbelief."[35] In our churches "we show the world a manner of life the world can never achieve through social coercion or governmental action," wrote Hauerwas and Willimon. "We serve the world by showing it something that it is not, namely, a place where God is forming a family out of strangers."[36] Christ has commissioned His churches to turn the world upside down with their optimistic love and see the kingdom come in men and women whose hearts are set ablaze by the message of grace.

Truly we are a people of destiny, watching for the return of Christ. The fellowship we enjoy with others of like faith in our churches is proof enough that we belong to this new creation movement, and we "meet with God when we meet with one another," wrote Peterson.[37] He further stated, "But this is only an anticipation of the ultimate reality, the fellowship of the heavenly city or 'the new Jerusalem', which will one day come down 'out of heaven from God' (Rev.

21:1–4)."[38] Our churches today are a preview of what the world will look like after the resurrection in the end, when the glory church fills the new earth. Let us upgrade our churches and the message to reflect the new instead of the old.

Living by God's love in our homes, churches, places of work, and whatever else we do, whether collecting stamps or mowing someone else's lawn, should show off the super-abundant life that Jesus came to offer everyone through grace. We are free at last. We know God personally.

Eden is no further from us believers today than our personal walk with God and the Christ-like love we live by every day. It is who we are, what we do, and how we feel about God, ourselves, and everyone we ever meet. Though the blessings of Eden will one day fill the whole earth with the glory of God in the end after the resurrection, today it is in our hearts, and it fills our churches and everything we do. Wherever there are people living like this, the glory that was lost in the Garden of Eden will have been restored, and God will live there too.

Nothing can beat this! Our consciences are new.

CHAPTER 7

An Invitation to Live by Love

Where Do We Go from Here?

The law and the prophets have served their purpose. They came to an end with the heralding ministry of John the Baptist, who was the forerunner of Christ. So say the Scriptures:

> "For all the prophets and the law prophesied until John."
>
> *Matt. 11:13 (Luke 16:16)*

It was John who would turn the pages of Scripture from prophecy to fulfillment. Thus the Old Testament had accomplished its purpose, and now it was time for the New Testament to take over and record the life and message of Jesus Christ the Son of God as the second Adam and the One Who gave birth to the new creation and established the Dispensation of Grace.

This is the story of Christianity and its message of love. At last friendship with God has been restored through the triumph of the cross, and the glory of loving oneness with Him has been made possible for all who believe. Eden's bliss is at hand.

Getting saved is all about a restored relationship with God. What was lost in the Garden of Eden was communion with their heavenly Father, which, with the successful mission of Christ, is given back to us in superabundance by His grace. This is why such terms as "forgiven," "delivered," "restored," "set free," "family," and "accepted in the Beloved," etc., mean so much to Christians. These terms, and so many others, have cleared the pathway to walk with God for the rest of your life, and in eternity to be one with Him forevermore. Getting saved says, "I want to know God personally and be restored to an intimate relationship with Him. I want to get rid of the stuff that is in the way, and I believe that Jesus is the only One Who can do this for me."

This is why the Christian mandate to live by love makes good sense—it is all about relationships.

The theme of the New Testament is the revelation of Christ, His cross, and the churches that were established by His disciples to gather His new creation into spiritual communities all over the world to show off their newfound relationship to God.

In practice those spiritual communities were outposts of heaven on earth, emulating the love between them and their Triune God. In theology they were the legacy of Christ's righteousness by grace through faith alone, enjoying a liberty that had not been experienced by man since before the fall in the Garden of Eden. In sacrifice they were examples of Christ's voluntary death, burial, and resurrection as they went about doing good and laying down their lives for others to see them saved, delivered, healed, and prospered in every area of their lives even as their souls prospered. In faith they were spiritual giants who believed the word of faith and readily turned the world upside down with their triumphant lifestyles of impossible feats in Jesus' name for the kingdom of God. In the Spirit they were as perfect as they would ever become, and they were bold about it, bearing the fruit of His fullness in their lives. In relationship they were the sanctified ones who enjoyed a personal walk with God and lived in communion with Him, looking forward to the day when He would be all in all in them. In hope they were His new creation who believed in a coming new heaven and new earth where they would enjoy pleasures at the right hand of God forevermore after the resurrection in the end.

They were never totally comfortable with living ordinary lives, as though man's mundane existence was all there was to life. They knew they were a people of destiny and expected more. Truly they believed that Jesus and the birthing of His new creation with His resurrection from the dead was the only door to such expectation. Therefore, they embraced eternity with one hand and time with the other, living the superabundant lives Jesus came to provide, not regarding the cost. "Grace, grace!" was their rallying cry.

They were full of the eternal life of God. Nothing could quench their living. They were spiritual and inspired the world with their passion for Christ's resurrection victory and His new creation. First century believers turned the world upside down. Their personal relationship with God was so real to them that it empowered them to face tremendous odds and sometimes even willingly pay the greatest price as they laid down their lives for their Savior.

Those spiritual communities were a grateful, singing, dancing people full of the Holy Spirit and His power, and they celebrated Jesus everywhere they went. They were God's Spirit-born, sanctified ones from the inside out. They had new consciences full of the love of God. Truth to them was found in a Person and not a worn out old religion and its laws. Furthermore, they were nothing like their old flesh that lay crucified in the grave with Christ. They looked to the risen Christ for their newness and had forgotten their past oldness. Growing from glory to glory was their quest.

With shouts of "grace, grace" they reigned in life and overcame the world, the flesh, and the devil. They were alive in the truest sense of the word. Jesus had done all of this for them back then, and He will also do it for you today if you so desire. As Tullian Tchividjian declared, "God's grace promises to give you a new beginning, a new purpose, a new destiny—if you'll stop running and allow him to set you free."[1]

Getting saved is about a restored relationship to God and accepting the offer of becoming a part of Christ's new creation, which is available to all. No one is too bad or too far gone or in too much trouble. No one is too high, too educated, or too important. Everyone is welcome. Jesus Himself taught that "no one, however low he may have fallen, is unable to receive the gift of the love of God, which God is longing to impart; the only condition being that the message shall be received by penitent hearts, with a childlike faith, which does not need to reason or to understand in order to receive a marvelous gift (Mark x. 15)," as Maurice Goguel wrote.[2] God's arms of love are open wide to receive you, and so are those new creation churches that are living by His love. How is this possible? The answer is found in one word—grace. Yes, God's undeserved, unexplainable, always available grace has made this so, and it will save anyone who believes and asks in Jesus' name.

God didn't look for great value in us, and Bender points out that God doesn't make us His people because we are already holy.[3] The good news is that the "real human being …is the object of the love of God," wrote Bonhoeffer.[4] We are all "worth looking for," as Henri Nouwen sums up many of Jesus' parables.[5] And Kreeft points out, God's love "is not dependent on our worth. It is not a response to our worth. It creates our worth.…God does it all, in Christ; we only have to accept it."[6]

"Is there room for me in Eden's new world of love?" you may be asking. The reply is always a resounding yes, if you believe that Jesus is the Son of God Who was sent by His heavenly Father to earth to show off His love for all by dying on the cross of Calvary for all our sins, and that He was raised from the dead on the third day, the firstborn, or prototype, of the new creation that He would save down through the centuries to the end.

Today Jesus is seated in heaven at His Father's right hand on a throne of grace, Lord over all on behalf of His churches, with the authority to save whoever calls on His name and enter into a personal relationship with them. Thank God for Jesus and His love for us all. Thank God for churches that are full of His love, enriching people's lives with the message of grace. As Ortberg declares, "If ever there were a true 'just as I am' church, if ever there were a community where everybody could bring all their baggage and brokenness with them without neat and tidy happy endings quite yet, if ever there was a group where everyone loved and no one pretended—we could not make enough room inside the building."[7]

Eden in this lifetime is best displayed in local churches, "in which the reality of the new creation is present, known, and experienced, and from which men and women will go into every sector of public life to claim it for Christ," as Newbigin stated.[8] They are built together by the Holy Spirit into temples of God where He communes with man—sanctuaries of love. Furthermore, "love enacted in community makes God known to the world.... Through our acts of love, the invisible God is made visible—palpable—among us," wrote Richard B. Hays of the church.[9] In no other relationships is God's love so empowered by the Holy Spirit to show off the glory of God and His coming kingdom in the end (Eph. 3:14–21). Thus it is "our task, as image-bearing, God-loving, Christ-shaped, Spirit-filled Christians, following Christ...to announce redemption to the world..., to announce healing to the world..., to proclaim love and trust to the world," declares N. T. Wright.[10]

And how did they go about doing this? They preached the ancient message of Christ ("the elementary principles of Christ," Heb. 6:1), which became the platform on which they built their new lives. These are the way of salvation taught by Jesus Christ's disciples. The Hebrew epistle sums up this beautiful message in chapter 6. It reveals the ABCs on being a Christian in the first century, and it is still so today.

> Therefore, leaving the discussion of the elementary principles of Christ, let us go on to perfection, not laying again the foundation of repentance from dead works and of faith toward God,

> of the doctrine of baptisms, of laying on of hands, of resurrection of the dead, and of eternal judgment.
> And this we will do if God permits.
>
> *Heb. 6:1–3*

Many respected authors agree that Hebrews 6 is consistent with the message and methods laid out in the book of Acts, the history book of early Christianity. I have quoted two authors below, from among many, for you to consider:

> This basic milk in the mind of our author includes elementary principles, that is, teaching basic doctrine: the foundation of repentance from dead works, faith toward God, the doctrine of baptisms, of laying on of hands, of resurrection of the dead, and of eternal judgment. Evidently, these were foundational elements of the faith taught by the catechists of the early church to the new converts; this was the milk.
>
> *Louis H. Evans, Jr.*[11]

> …even before the end of the first century A.D., there were certain truths which were regularly put before enquirers and young Christians, forming an outline of teaching, already becoming traditional, offered to catechumens. Quite clearly there would have been no purpose in the mention of these particular points, unless they were familiar, both to writer and to readers, as forming the A B C of Christian doctrine.
>
> *Theodore H. Robinson*[12]

It is exciting to find out that you can be saved and restored to fellowship with God and His people, the way they were in the first century, and rest assured that you will not go to hell, but rather to heaven when you die, and in the end live with Christ on a new earth in new heavens.

It is also just as rewarding to know that today God wants to add you to the church body of His choosing, to serve out your earthly priesthood (1 Pet. 2:5; 1 Cor. 12:18–31) as you learn to live by love. It is there that you will be empowered to grow up practically into the image of Christ (Rom. 8:29; Col. 3:10), and thus successfully pursue the call of God on your life (Rom. 12:1–8) to show off Jesus and the fellowship you enjoy with Him to the world.

This is what church life is all about. This is God's design for this Dispensation of Grace. In the Old Testament God's people formed a physical nation located in the Middle East, centered in Jerusalem. Today they form a worldwide spiritual nation centered in their churches. It took me a long time to sort these issues out, because our mainline denomination never taught them. Thank God those days of ignorance are over. What a joy it is for me to be able to share them fully with you.

This is the grace message in a nutshell: Christ, His cross, and His church. This is what getting saved is all about, and Heb. 6:1–3 lays out the basic truths they introduced and built their Christian faith on. The bottom line is this: God wants to restore your relationship to Him by making you a part of His new creation family and thus giving your life true meaning. Thank God we can know these things in our "knower" and live God-inspired lives that show off our close relationship with Him.

Let us review the ABCs on how to become a Christian and enjoy a personal relationship with Him. As I have already said, the most succinct and easy-to-understand directive is found in Hebrews 6:1,2. These six are the foundational, elementary principles, on becoming a Christian in this Dispensation of Grace.

The Six Foundational Principles

These six foundation principles easily divide themselves into three pairs: First, *A new start with God*. Next, *A new life with God and His people*. Last, *A new vision of God's world today and tomorrow.*

1. *A new start with God*

> …not laying again the foundation of **repentance** from dead works and of **faith** toward God,
>
> *Heb. 6:1*

Christian, your salvation is all about Jesus and none other. He alone is the way to return to fellowship with God. It is He Who died on the cross of Calvary for all sin to achieve this, and was raised from the dead to offer forgiveness and His righteousness by grace to all who wish to turn from their sinful living and call upon Him to be saved by faith. He alone can give you the new creation start in life you need to become a member of God's family. This new start is how your lost communion with God is restored. And it is all about the grace of God to give you the **repentance** (change of mind) and **faith** (believing in your heart) you need to receive Jesus Christ as your Lord and Savior and thus be born again by the Holy Spirit.

= **By grace I turn from sin and receive Jesus as my Lord and Savior by faith.**

> "Truly, these times of ignorance God overlooked, but
> now commands all men everywhere to **repent**,
> because He has appointed a day on which He will judge the world in righteousness by the Man whom He has ordained. He has given assurance of this to all by raising Him from the dead."
>
> *Acts 17:30,31*

> "how I kept back nothing that was helpful, but proclaimed it to you, and taught you publicly and from house to house,
> testifying to Jews, and also to Greeks, **repentance** toward God and **faith** toward our Lord Jesus Christ."
>
> *Acts 20:20,21*

> that if you confess with your mouth the Lord Jesus and **believe** in your heart that God has raised Him from the dead, you will be saved.
> For with the heart one **believes** unto righteousness, and with the mouth confession is made unto salvation.
>
> *Rom. 10:9,10*

> For by grace you have been saved through **faith**, and that not of yourselves; it is the gift of God,
> not of works, lest anyone should boast.
>
> *Eph. 2:8,9*

2. *A new life with God and His people*

> of the doctrine of baptisms, of laying on of hands,…
>
> *Heb. 6:2a*

Having your relationship restored to God is the most important thing that can happen to anyone. It sets you up to be led by His Spirit and live a powerful, positive life full of hope. Now that Jesus is your Lord and Savior, it is time for you to submit yourself as a candidate for believer's **baptism.** Getting saved is a private matter between you and God; getting **baptized** in water is a public matter that identifies you with Christ and the people of God. Both are very important. After **baptism** believers are anointed with the gift of the Holy Spirit, usually through the **laying on of hands** upon reception into the church body. This gift gives believers the power they need to live for Christ and minister the spiritual gifts. After salvation, nothing is more life-changing for the new creation than these.

= By faith I submit to believer's baptism into the church body, and through the laying on of hands I receive the gift of the Holy Spirit for service.

> Now as they went down the road, they came to some water. And the eunuch said, "See, here is water. What hinders me from being **baptized**?"
> Then Philip said, "If you believe with all your heart, you may." And he answered and said, "I believe that Jesus Christ is the Son of God."
> So he commanded the chariot to stand still. And both Philip and the eunuch went down into the water, and he **baptized** him.
>
> *Acts 8:36–38*

> Then Peter said to them, "Repent, and let every one of you be **baptized** in the name of Jesus Christ for the remission of sins; and you shall receive **the gift of the Holy Spirit**.
> For the promise is to you and to your children, and to all who are afar off, as many as the Lord our God will call."
>
> *Acts 2:38,39*

> When they heard this, they were baptized in the name of the Lord Jesus.

> And when Paul had **laid hands** on them, the Holy Spirit came upon them, and they spoke with tongues and prophesied.
>
> *Acts 19:5,6*

3. *A new vision of God's world today and tomorrow*

> ...of resurrection of the dead, and of eternal judgment.
>
> *Heb. 6:2b*

One of the most shocking discoveries I made after I was saved was that this world was not really my home, and that in the **resurrection** I would rise up made alive by the Holy Spirit like Jesus and join Him on a new earth in new heavens forevermore. This was my destiny in Christ. What a thrill! I have not come down off that high since the day I first heard about the **resurrection** from the dead. This has colored my worldview. Truly His love for me has become my motivation.

At last I know what my destiny is all about, and I live every day with this future in mind. There is something else that I never forget: the coming **judgment** that the world faces because they have rejected Jesus Christ as their Lord and Savior. What a terrible day that will be for them! What unnecessary loss! Hell was made for satan and his rebellious angels (Matt. 25:41); don't join them by making the same mistake they did in rebelling against God.

In contrast, I thank Him every day that for His new creation this will be the happiest day of our lives, because Jesus has already taken our judgment on Himself on the cross. It is there that we will be rewarded for living a life of love and faith as we have reigned in life through Christ's grace in the power of the Spirit. A new heaven and a new earth await us with pleasures at the right hand of God forevermore.

= By faith I live in anticipation of looking like Christ in the resurrection and the final judgment, when the saved will receive their rewards and the unfortunate unbelievers will be cast into the lake of fire forever.

Beloved, now we are children of God; and it has not yet been revealed what we shall be, but we know that when He is **revealed**, we shall be like Him, for we shall see Him as He is.

1 John 3:2

For I am already being poured out as a drink offering, and the time of my departure is at hand.
I have fought the good fight, I have finished the race, I have kept the faith.
Finally, there is laid up for me the crown of righteousness, which the Lord, the righteous Judge, will give to

me on that Day, and not to me only but also to all who have loved His appearing.

2 Tim. 4:6–8

Therefore we make it our aim, whether present or absent, to be well pleasing to Him.
For we must all appear before the **judgment** seat of Christ, that each one may receive the things done in the body, according to what he has done, whether good or bad.
Knowing, therefore, the terror of the Lord, we persuade men; but we are well known to God, and I also trust are well known in your consciences.

2 Cor. 5:9–11

I know you believe this New Testament record and want to be saved. Pray this prayer right now by faith and God will save you by grace, and Eden's love and a new relationship with God will be yours forevermore:

"Loving Heavenly Father, I do believe that Jesus is the Savior of the world Who died on the cross of Calvary for everyone's sin, including mine, and that He rose from the dead on the third day so that my relationship to You could be restored. I know He is at Your right hand in heaven today, Lord over all on behalf of His churches. By faith I repent of my sins and receive You, Jesus, as my Lord and Savior.

> "Thank You for hearing my prayer and saving me and bringing me to the church of Your choosing, where You will baptize me in water, anoint me with your Spirit, and add me to that new creation fellowship of love as I await Your return."

At last Eden's precious relationship with God has been restored in Christ's new creation and their churches, and it is only a matter of time before their love fills the new heavens and new earth.

GLOSSARY

advent. The incarnation or birth of Christ in Bethlehem, which we celebrate at Christmas ("Advent" or the "first advent"). Also, the second coming of Christ in the end at the resurrection (the "second advent").

agapé, agapē. Of the four Greek words for love, *agapē* refers specifically to divine love, God's love, the highest form of love, under which the other three types (brotherly love, sensual love, appreciation) reach their highest potential. *Agapē* is the love spoken of in the expression "Calvary love," that is, the absolute love of God displayed by Jesus on the cross of Calvary and by the Spirit in His churches.

anointed. So named for the sacred rite of anointing someone with oil for consecration. Also, to be chosen, empowered, or taught by the Holy Spirit.

arrabon, arrabōn. The Greek word translated as "earnest" in the King James Version of the Bible, and as "guarantee" in the NKJV. Found in 2 Cor. 1:22; 5:5; Eph. 1:14. See "earnest."

archetype, archetypal. The original pattern or model of which all things of the same type are representations or copies; see "prototype."

believer-priest. The position and function of every believer in the churches of God, as described, for example, in 1 Pet. 2:5–9; see "priesthood."

born again. Having experienced the new birth by becoming a Christian. Also known as being "spiritually reborn" or "born from above" by the Spirit of God (John 3:3–8).

carnal. According to the life of the unregenerate, human flesh; see "flesh."

cosmos. A universal arrangement or ordered system. The "world" in the New Testament: may refer to the earth, or to the system of life on the earth. "God so loved the world" (Gk. *kosmos*; John 3:16) that He gave His Son Jesus to save whoever would believe in Him. Believers are not to be "conformed to this world" (*kosmos*; Rom. 8:29). The "form of this world is passing away" (*kosmos*; 1 Cor. 7:30).

counterculture. A way of life and set of attitudes opposed to or at variance with the prevailing social norm. The new creation is a counterculture, as it does not fit in with the life of the old creation or cosmos.

covenant. An agreement that brings about a relationship of commitment between God and his people. "Old Covenant" or "Law Covenant" refers to the covenant between God and Israel under the Law of Moses. "New Covenant" or "Grace Covenant" refers to the covenant between God and the followers of His Son Jesus Christ.

dead works. Works performed according to the flesh, whether good or bad, for God or self. By the Spirit of God, Christians are "cleansed from dead works to serve the living God," not their old nature (Heb. 9:14; 6:1).

dispensation. An administration, government, economy, or system of revealed commands, promises, and conditions regulating human affairs and God's dealings with man, as in "the law dispensation" or "the Dispensation of Grace."

earnest. A token or pledge of what is to come; down payment or guarantee to bind a transaction; see "*arrabōn*."

ecclesiology. The study of Christ's churches.

eschatology. The study of last things, or Bible prophecy, including the present age since the birth of Christ, and all that will transpire with His second coming and beyond.

firstfruits. The earliest gathered fruit, as a sign or promise of the rest of the harvest to come. In the New Testament, this term was applied to Christ (1 Cor. 15:20,23), the Holy Spirit (Rom. 8:23), and believers (Jas. 1:18).

flesh. Everything about people that is contrary to God's design or God's way of living by the Spirit; as in the expression "according to the flesh." Contained in the word "carnal." It speaks of the old, sinful, crucified nature.

grace. The generous, unmerited favor of God.

justification. The status of being legally cleared of wrongdoing and declared righteous in the sight of God.

law. Generally, the whole body of rules binding the customs or practices of a community, or enforced by a controlling authority. Specifically, as used in this book, "the law" refers to the law of Moses, including the Ten Commandments and all the ceremonial and civil laws as set forth in the Old Testament; it may also refer to any set of legal requirements, or dos and don'ts, for trying to obtain or maintain a righteous standing with

God or earn His favor. In this sense, law and grace cannot mix.

legalistic. Consisting of or governed by a specific set of laws or requirements, whether real or contrived; see "law."

local church. An expression that emphasizes the tangible nature of Christ's churches, or assemblies, that meet at a specific location, contrary to any concept of a universal church, visible or invisible, as developed in some denominations.

messianic, Messianic. Relating to Jesus the Messiah, the promised, anointed Savior of the people of God.

new creation. The new, or second, creation established by Christ at His resurrection, as the ultimate replacement for the original creation that was ruined by the disobedience of Adam and Eve in the Garden of Eden. While the present, old creation will continue to the end, Christians enjoy the life of the new creation in foretaste, awaiting the full manifestation of the new creation at the resurrection in the end, and the passing away of the old creation. If anyone is in Christ, there is "new creation" (2 Cor. 5:17; Gal. 6:15). Christ is the firstborn over the new creation (Col. 1:15; Rev. 1:5; see "prototype").

priesthood. Under the Old Covenant, that select class of men who were allowed to serve in the temple and intercede before God on behalf of the people of Israel. Under the New Covenant, Jesus has become the great High Priest for all believers (Heb. 4:14; 6:19,20; 8:1), and the function of priesthood has been passed on to all believers to serve in the house of God, the local church. See "believer-priest."

prophetic. The nature of hearing and receiving revelation from God, and the quality of living according to and speaking that same type of word from Him, the "now" word. All believers may prophesy (1 Cor. 14:31): "But he who prophesies speaks edification and exhortation and comfort to men" (1 Cor. 14:3).

prototype. First of a type or kind, from which others of the same type are developed or copied. Derived from the concept of the Greek word *prōtotokos*, or "firstborn," referring directly to Jesus as the firstborn, or prototype, of the new creation (Rom. 8:29; Col. 1:15).

resurrection of believers. All believers rising from the dead at the end of this age upon the return of Christ, which some refer to as the "rapture" of the saved, when "the trumpet will sound, and the dead will be raised incorruptible, and we shall be changed" (1 Cor. 15:52).

saint. The most popular word used in the New Testament to refer to Christians; one who has been "set apart" or "sanctified" by becoming a Christian. Used 62 times in the New Testament, speaking of all believers in any given location.

salvation, saved, getting saved. The one-time process of repentance and faith whereby a person is born again. The hope of every believer, "kept by the power of God through faith for salvation ready to be revealed in the last time" (1 Pet. 1:5).

sanctification. The quality of being set apart, declared holy, or consecrated. See "saint."

scapegoat. In the Old Testament, a goat sent into the wilderness after the chief priest had symbolically laid the sins of the people upon it (Lev. 16). It was a type of Christ (see "type").

shadow, type. A representation or copy of the real thing, but lacking its substance; a foreshadowing in the Old Testament of a person or event to come in the New Testament, which fulfills the Law Covenant with all of its ceremonies and observances (Col. 2:16,17; Heb. 8:5; 10:1).

triune. Consisting of three in one, specifically of the Trinity of the Godhead—the Father, the Son, and the Holy Spirit.

type. As in the expression "shadows and types"; see "shadow."

ungrace. The opposite of grace; the complete absence of grace.

unlove. The opposite of God's *agapē* love; the world's love.

unregenerate. Not a Christian, never having experienced the new birth in Christ; see "born again."

BIBLIOGRAPHY

Achtemeier, Paul J. *1 Peter*. Minneapolis: Fortress Press, 1996.

Alexander, T. Desmond. *From Eden to the New Jerusalem*. Grand Rapids: Kregel Academic & Professional, 2008.

Banks, Robert. *Paul's Idea of Community*. Exeter: The Paternoster Press, 1980.

Bannerman, James. *The Church of Christ*, Vol. 1. Carlisle, PA: The Banner of Truth Trust, 1960.

Barth, Markus. *Conversation with the Bible*. New York: Holt, Rinehart and Winston, 1964.

Beale, G. K. *The Temple and the Church's Mission*. Downers Grove, IL: InterVarsity Press, 2004.

Beasley-Murray, G. R. *Jesus and the Kingdom of God*. Grand Rapids: William B. Eerdmans Publishing Company, 1986.

Bender, Harold S. *These Are My People*. Scottdale, PA: Herald Press, 1962.

Best, Ernest. *One Body in Christ*. London: S.P.C.K., 1955.

Bolton, Samuel. *The True Bounds of Christian Freedom*. Carlisle, PA: The Banner of Truth Trust, 1964.

Bonhoeffer, Dietrich. *Creation and Fall*. Trans. by Douglas Stephen Bax. Minneapolis: Fortress Press, 1997.

———. *Ethics*. Trans. by Reinhard Krauss, Charles C. West, and Douglas W. Stott. Minneapolis: Fortress Press, 2005.

Booth, Abraham. *The Reign of Grace*. Darlington, England: Evangelical Press, 2003.

Boyd, Gregory A. *Repenting of Religion*. Grand Rapids: Baker Books, 2004.

Bray, Gerald. *God Is Love*. Wheaton, IL: Crossway, 2012.

Bright, John. *The Kingdom of God*. Nashville: Abingdon Press, 1981.

Brunner, Emil. *The Mediator*. Trans. by Olive Wyon. Philadelphia: The Westminster Press, 1947.

Clapp, Rodney. *A Peculiar People*. Downers Grove, IL: InterVarsity Press, 1996.

Coppedge, Allan. *The God Who Is Triune*. Downers Grove, IL: IVP Academic, 2007.

Cullmann, Oscar. *The Christology of the New Testament*. Trans. by Shirley C. Guthrie and Charles A. M. Hall. Philadelphia: Westminster Press, 1963.

———. *Salvation in History*. Trans. by Sidney G. Sowers. New York: Harper & Row, Publishers, 1967.

Dever, Mark. *Nine Marks of a Healthy Church*. Wheaton, IL: Crossway Books, 2004.

———. *What Is a Healthy Church?* Wheaton, IL: Crossway Books, 2007.

Dubis, Mark. *I Peter: A Handbook on the Greek Text*. Waco, TX: Baylor University Press, 2010.

Dunn, James D. G. *The Theology of Paul the Apostle*. Grand Rapids: William B. Eerdmans Publishing Company, 1998.

Elliott, John H. *I Peter*. New Haven: Yale University Press, 2000.

Ellis, E. Earle. *Paul's Use of the Old Testament*. Grand Rapids: William B. Eerdmans Publishing Company, 1957.

Evans, Louis H. Evans, Jr. *Hebrews*. Waco, TX: Word Books, Publishers, 1985.

Fee, Gordon D. *God's Empowering Presence*. Grand Rapids: Baker Academic, 2011.

Flew, R. Newton. *Jesus and His Church*. London: The Epworth Press, 1943.

Fridrichsen, Anton. "Jesus, St John and St Paul," in *The Root of the Vine*. New York: Philosophical Library, 1953.

Gillquist, Peter E. *Why We Haven't Changed the World*. Old Tappan, NJ: Fleming H. Revell Company, 1982.

Goguel, Maurice. *The Life of Jesus*. Trans. by Olive Wyon. London: George Allen & Unwin Ltd, 1953.

Grenz, Stanley J. *Created for Community*. Grand Rapids: Baker Academic, 1998.

Gunton, Colin E. *The One, the Three and the Many*. Cambridge: Cambridge University Press, 1993.

———. *The Triune Creator*. Grand Rapids: William B. Eerdmans Publishing Company, 1998.

Habig, Brian and Newsom, Les. *The Enduring Community*. Jackson, MS: Reformed University Press, 2001.

Hanigan, James P. "Conscience and the Holy Spirit," in *Conscience*. Ed. by Charles E. Curran. New York: Paulist Press, 2004.

Harris, Murray J. *Raised Immortal*. Grand Rapids: William B. Eerdmans Publishing Company, 1983.

Hauerwas, Stanley and Willimon, William H. *Resident Aliens*. Nashville: Abingdon Press, 1989.

Hays, Richard B. *The Moral Vision of the New Testament.* New York: HarperOne, 1996.

Hendry, George S. *The Gospel of the Incarnation.* Philadelphia: The Westminster Press, 1958.

Hoekema, Anthony A. *The Bible and the Future.* Grand Rapids: William B. Eerdmans Publishing Company, 1979.

Hulse, Erroll. *The Testimony of Baptism.* Sussex, England: Carey Publications, 1982.

Johnson, Darrell W. *Experiencing the Trinity.* Vancouver: Regent College Publishing, 2002.

Jukes, Andrew. *The Names of God.* Grand Rapids: Kregel Publications, 1967.

Käsemann, Ernst. *Jesus Means Freedom.* Trans. by Frank Clarke. Minneapolis: Fortress Press, 2007.

Kline, Meredith G. *God, Heaven, and Har Magedon.* Eugene, OR: Wipf & Stock Publishers, 2006. Used by permission of Wipf and Stock Publishers. www.wipfandstock.com

———. *Images of the Spirit.* Eugene, OR: Wipf & Stock Publishers, 1999. Used by permission of Wipf and Stock Publishers. www.wipfandstock.com

Kreeft, Peter. *The God Who Loves You.* San Francisco: Ignatius Press, 2004.

Ladd, George Eldon. *The Gospel of the Kingdom.* Grand Rapids: William B. Eerdmans Publishing Company, 1959.

———. *The Presence of the Future.* Grand Rapids: William B. Eerdmans Publishing Company, 1974.

Leithart, Peter J. *The Kingdom and the Power.* Phillipsburg, NJ: P&R Publishing, 1993.

Letham, Robert. *The Holy Trinity*. Phillipsburg, NJ: P&R Publishing, 2004.

Lewis, C. S. *The Four Loves*. New York: Harcourt Brace & Company, 1988.

———. *The Problem of Pain*. New York: HarperSanFrancisco, 1996.

Lincoln, Andrew T. *Paradise Now and Not Yet*. Cambridge: Cambridge University Press, 1981.

Lloyd-Jones, Martyn. *Life in Christ: Studies in 1 John*. Wheaton, IL: Crossway Books, 2002.

Lohmeyer, Ernst. *Lord of the Temple*. Trans. by Stewart Todd. Richmond, VA: John Knox Press, 1961.

Mackintosh, H. R. *The Christian Experience of Forgiveness*. New York: Harper & Brothers Publishers, 1927.

Manson, William. *Jesus and the Christian*. Grand Rapids: William B. Eerdmans Publishing Company, 1967.

———. *Jesus the Messiah*. London: Hodder and Stoughton Ltd., 1943.

McCallum, Dennis. *Walking in Victory*. Columbus, OH: Xenos Publishing, 2002.

McKelvey, R. J. *The New Temple*. London: Oxford University Press, 1969.

Middleton, J. Richard. *A New Heaven and a New Earth*. Grand Rapids: Baker Academic, 2014.

Milbank, John. *Theology and Social Theory*. Oxford: Blackwell Publishers Ltd., 1993.

Minear, Paul Sevier. *Christians and the New Creation*. Louisville: Westminster John Knox Press, 1994.

———. *Jesus and His People*. New York: Association Press, 1956.

Moltmann, Jürgen. *The Trinity and the Kingdom*. Trans. by Margaret Kohl. Minneapolis: Fortress Press, 1993.

Newbigin, Lesslie. *The Gospel in a Pluralist Society*. Grand Rapids: William B. Eerdmans Publishing Company, 1989.

———. *The Household of God*. Eugene, OR: Wipf and Stock Publishers, 2008.

Nouwen, Henri J. M. *The Return of the Prodigal Son*. New York: Image Books, 1994.

Ortberg, John. *Love Beyond Reason*. Grand Rapids: Zondervan, 1998.

———. *The Me I Want to Be*. Grand Rapids: Zondervan, 2010.

Otto, Rudolf. *The Kingdom of God and the Son of Man*. Trans. by Floyd V. Filson and Bertram Lee-Woolf. Boston: Starr King Press, 1957.

Peterson, David. *Engaging with God*. Downers Grove, IL: InterVarsity Press, 1992.

———. *Possessed by God*. Downers Grove, IL: InterVarsity Press, 1995.

Pieters, Albertus. *The Seed of Abraham*. William B. Eerdmans Publishing Company, 1950.

Richter, Sandra L. *The Epic of Eden*. Downers Grove, IL: IVP Academic, 2008.

Ridderbos, Herman. *The Coming of the Kingdom*. Trans. by H. de Jongste. Philadelphia: Presbyterian and Reformed Publishing Company, 1962.

Robinson, Theodore H. *The Epistle to the Hebrews*. London: Hodder and Stoughton, 1933.

Schaeffer, Francis. *True Spirituality*. Carol Stream, IL: Tyndale House Publishers, 2001.

Schweizer, Eduard. *The Holy Spirit.* Trans. by Reginald H. and Ilse Fuller. London: SCM Press Ltd., 1981.

Scott, E. F. *The Kingdom and the Messiah.* Edinburgh: T. & T. Clark, 1911.

Shelley, Bruce L. *The Church: God's People.* Wheaton, IL: Victor Books, 1978.

Sittler, Joseph. *Essays on Nature and Grace.* Philadelphia: Fortress Press, 1972.

Smith, James Bryan. *Embracing the Love of God.* New York: HarperOne, 1995.

Snyder, Howard A. *The Community of the King.* Downers Grove, IL: IVP Academic. 2004.

Sproul, R. C. *Faith Alone.* Grand Rapids: Baker Books, 1995.

Steere, David. *Bodily Expressions in Psychotherapy.* New York: Brunner/Mazel, Publishers, 1982.

Tannehill, Robert C. *Dying and Rising with Christ.* Eugene, OR: Wipf & Stock Publishers, 2006. Used by permission of Wipf and Stock Publishers. www.wipfandstock.com

Tchividjian, Tullian. *Surprised by Grace.* Wheaton, IL: Crossway, 2010.

Thornton, L. S. *Christ and the Church.* Westminster: Dacre Press, 1956.

———. *The Common Life in the Body of Christ.* Westminster: Dacre Press, 1944.

———. *The Dominion of Christ.* Westminster: Dacre Press, 1952.

Torrance, Thomas F. *The Christian Doctrine of God.* London: T&T Clark Ltd., 2001. An imprint of Bloomsbury Publishing Plc.

Tournier, Paul. *Guilt and Grace*. Trans. by Arthur W. Heathcote. New York: Harper & Row, Publishers, 1962.

Trites, Allison A. "Witness and the Resurrection in the Apocalypse of John," in *Life in the Face of Death*. Ed. by Richard N. Longenecker. Grand Rapids: William B. Eerdmans Publishing Company, 1998.

Vos, Geerhardus. *The Pauline Eschatology*. Phillipsburg, NJ: P&R Publishing, 1994.

Welch, Claude. *The Reality of the Church*. New York: Charles Scribner's Sons, 1958.

Wells, David F. *Above All Earthly Pow'rs*. Grand Rapids: William B. Eerdmans Publishing Company, 2005.

Westley, Dick. *Redemptive Intimacy*. Mystic, CT: Twenty-Third Publications, 1981.

Whitney, Donald S. *Spiritual Disciplines Within the Church*. Chicago: Moody Publishers, 1996.

Wilmot, John. *Inspired Principles of Prophetic Interpretation*. Swengel, PA: Reiner Publications, 1975.

Wink, Walter. *Engaging the Powers*. Minneapolis: Fortress Press, 1992.

Wright, N. T. *The Challenge of Easter*. Downers Grove, IL: IVP Books, 2009.

———. *Following Jesus*. Grand Rapids: William B. Eerdmans Publishing Company, 1995.

———. *The Resurrection of the Son of God*. Minneapolis: Fortress Press, 2003.

———. *Surprised by Hope*. New York: HarperOne, 2008.

Yoder, John Howard. *The Politics of Jesus*. Grand Rapids: William B. Eerdmans Publishing Company, 1994.

———. *The Royal Priesthood*. Scottdale, PA: Herald Press, 1998.

NOTES

CHAPTER 1
The Need to Return to Eden
A Beginning

1. Stanley J. Grenz, *Created for Community*, 61.
2. Colin E. Gunton, *The Triune Creator*, 9.
3. Thomas F. Torrance, *The Christian Doctrine of God, One Being Three Persons*, 244.
4. Gerald Bray, *God Is Love: A Biblical and Systematic Theology*, 524.
5. Robert Letham, *The Holy Trinity*, 428.
6. Gregory A. Boyd, *Repenting of Religion*, 66.
7. Torrance, 240–241.
8. T. Desmond Alexander, *From Eden to the New Jerusalem*, 78.
9. Jürgen Moltmann, *The Trinity and the Kingdom*, 106.
10. Torrance, 245.
11. Peter Kreeft, *The God Who Loves You*, 53.
12. Torrance, 59.
13. Alexander, 78.
14. Bray, 347.

15. Boyd, 126.
16. G. K. Beale, *The Temple and the Church's Mission*, 66.
17. Paul Tournier, *Guilt & Grace*, 148.
18. Sandra L. Richter, *The Epic of Eden*, 114.
19. Meredith G. Kline, *God, Heaven, and Har Magedon*, 22. Used by permission of Wipf and Stock Publishers. www.wipfandstock.com
20. C. S. Lewis, *The Problem of Pain*, 80.
21. Grenz, 79.
22. Murray J. Harris, *Raised Immortal*, 168.
23. Boyd, 158.
24. Bray, 375.
25. Allan Coppedge, *The God Who Is Triune*, 278.
26. Henri J. M. Nouwen, *The Return of the Prodigal Son*, 129.
27. Coppedge, 278.
28. Kreeft, 116.
29. Lewis, 155.
30. Bray, 374.
31. Nouwen, 43.
32. Bray, 94.
33. Ibid., 374.
34. Oscar Cullmann, *Salvation in History*, 256.
35. Alexander, 79.
36. John Howard Yoder, *The Politics of Jesus*, 141.
37. Richter, 134.
38. Ibid., 219.
39. Anthony A. Hoekema, *The Bible and the Future*, 287.

CHAPTER 2
The Day After Their Disobedience
A Legacy of Criticism

1. Grenz, 92.
2. Boyd, 147.
3. Richter, 104.
4. Paul Minear, *Christians and the New Creation*, 39.
5. L. S. Thornton, *The Dominion of Christ*, 80.
6. Boyd, 147.
7. Lewis, 73.
8. Grenz, 93.
9. Ibid.
10. Minear, 25.
11. Tournier, 74.
12. Richter, 115.
13. Dietrich Bonhoeffer, *Creation and Fall*, 127.
14. Lewis, 63.
15. Grenz, 93.
16. Lewis, 79.
17. Meredith G. Kline, *Images of the Spirit*, 31. Used by permission of Wipf and Stock Publishers. www.wipfandstock.com
18. Thornton, 79.
19. Ibid., 131.
20. James D. G. Dunn, *The Theology of Paul the Apostle*, 94.
21. Grenz, 93.
22. Torrance, 226.
23. Kline, *Images of the Spirit*, 32.

CHAPTER 3

Christ, the Second Adam

A New Creation

1. N. T. Wright, *The Challenge of Easter*, 46.
2. Coppedge, 116.
3. Lesslie Newbigin, *The Gospel in a Pluralist Society*, 175.
4. N. T. Wright, *The Resurrection of the Son of God*, 341.
5. Grenz, 122.
6. Dunn, 468.
7. E. Earle Ellis, *Paul's Use of the Old Testament*, 129.
8. Yoder, *The Politics of Jesus*, 185.
9. John Howard Yoder, *The Royal Priesthood*, 126
10. Eduard Schweizer, *The Holy Spirit*, 68.
11. William Manson, *Jesus and the Christian*, 110.
12. Thornton, *The Dominion of Christ*.
13. Manson, 189.
14. Ernst Käsemann, *Jesus Means Freedom*, 76.
15. Mark Dubis, *I Peter: A Handbook on the Greek Text*, 35.
16. Paul J. Achtemeier, *1 Peter*, 135.
17. Yoder, *The Royal Priesthood*, 117.
18. R. J. McKelvey, *The New Temple*, 154.
19. Walter Wink, *Engaging the Powers*, 70.
20. Torrance, 214.
21. Robert C. Tannehill, *Dying and Rising with Christ*, 27.
22. Yoder, *The Royal Priesthood*, 74.
23. Manson, 104.
24. Brian Habig and Les Newsom, *The Enduring Community*, 137.
25. Mark Dever, *What Is a Healthy Church?*, 29.

26. Lesslie Newbigin, *The Household of God*, 130. Used by permission of Wipf and Stock Publishers. www.wipfandstock.com

27. Manson, 97.

CHAPTER 4
Back to Eden and the Good Life
With Shouts of "Grace, Grace!"

1. John Wilmot, *Inspired Principles of Prophetic Interpretation*, 45.
2. Manson, 93.
3. Coppedge, 117.
4. G. R. Beasley-Murray, *Jesus and the Kingdom of God*, 339.
5. Kline, *God, Heaven, and Har Magedon*, 20.
6. Beale, 170.
7. Darrell W. Johnson, *Experiencing the Trinity*, 67.
8. Bonhoeffer, 128.
9. Schweizer, 86.
10. Käsemann, 25.
11. Thornton, 4.
12. Martyn Lloyd-Jones, *Life in Christ*, 244.
13. Newbigin, *The Household of God*, 92.
14. Wright, *The Resurrection of the Son of God*, 342.
15. Dick Westley, *Redemptive Intimacy*, 134–135.
16. Schweizer, 83.

CHAPTER 5
Experiencing God's Love
Real Christians Love like Jesus

1. Grenz, 48.

2. Moltmann, 106.
3. Torrance, 209.
4. Grenz, 80.
5. Ibid., 47.
6. Wink, 269.
7. Ernst Lohmeyer, *Lord of the Temple*, 100–101.
8. William Manson, *Jesus the Messiah*, 83. Reproduced by permission of Hodder and Stoughton Limited.
9. Anton Fridrichsen, "Jesus, St John and St Paul," in *The Root of the Vine*, 46.
10. Westley, 117.
11. Johnson, 78.
12. Paul Minear, *Jesus and His People*, 31.
13. Johnson, 78.
14. Manson, *Jesus and the Christian*, 193.
15. Schweizer, 93.
16. Fee, 214.
17. Westley, 57.
18. Ibid., 61.
19. C. S. Lewis, *The Four Loves*, 121.
20. Schweizer, 69.
21. Gunton, 202.
22. Oscar Cullmann, *The Christology of the New Testament*, 172.
23. Beale, 173.
24. Maurice Goguel, *The Life of Jesus*, 110.
25. Coppedge, 120.
26. Gordon D. Fee, *God's Empowering Presence*, 496.
27. Thornton, 4.

28. Allison A. Trites, "Witness and the Resurrection in the Apocalypse of John," in *Life in the Face of Death*, 282.
29. Moltmann, 56.
30. George S. Hendry, *The Gospel of the Incarnation*, 135.
31. Richter, 216.
32. Harris, 125.
33. Herman Ridderbos, *The Coming of the Kingdom*, 274.
34. Kreeft, 31.
35. Fee, 497.
36. Johnson, 63.
37. Markus Barth, *Conversation with the Bible*, 9–10.
38. Bonhoeffer, 125.
39. Moltmann, 57.
40. John Ortberg, *Love Beyond Reason*, 52.
41. Albertus Pieters, *The Seed of Abraham*, 66.
42. Grenz, 231–232.
43. James Bannerman, *The Church of Christ*, Vol. 1, 18–19.
44. Fridrichsen, 60.
45. Grenz, 79.
46. Robert Banks, *Paul's Idea of Community*, 33.
47. Bannerman, 20–21.
48. Colin E. Gunton, *The One, the Three and the Many*, 223.
49. Andrew Jukes, *The Names of God*, 177.
50. Coppedge, 118.
51. Thornton, 14.
52. Manson, *Jesus and the Christian*, 102.
53. Torrance, 210.
54. Käsemann, 57.
55. Howard A. Snyder, *The Community of the King*, 91.

56. Erroll Hulse, *The Testimony of Baptism*, 79.
57. Banks, 76.
58. Peter J. Leithart, *The Kingdom and the Power*, 164.
59. Bray, 309.
60. Kreeft, 107.
61. Westley, 99.
62. James Bryan Smith, *Embracing the Love of God*, 148.
63. Snyder, 85.
64. Smith, 75.
65. Nouwen, 106.
66. Hendry, 133.
67. Ortberg, 193.
68. Ibid., 188.
69. Snyder, 91.
70. Harold S. Bender, *These Are My People*, 47.
71. Leithart, 165.
72. Stanley Hauerwas and William H. Willimon, *Resident Aliens*, 49.
73. Newbigin, *The Household of God*, 143.
74. Banks, 47.
75. L. S. Thornton, *The Common Life in the Body of Christ*, 312–313.
76. David Peterson, *Possessed by God*, 32.
77. Yoder, *The Politics of Jesus*, 222.
78. Fee, 447.

CHAPTER 6
A Perfect Conscience Full of Love
Back to Eden Today

1. Bonhoeffer, 122.
2. Boyd, 109.
3. Tournier, 74–75.
4. Ortberg, 132.
5. Peterson, 49.
6. Hauerwas and Willimon, 77.
7. Manson, *Jesus and the Christian*, 221.
8. John Ortberg, *The Me I Want to Be*, 119.
9. Boyd, 30.
10. Thornton, *The Dominion of Christ*, 5.
11. L. S. Thornton, *Christ and the Church*, 50. See also, for example, R. J. McKelvey, *The New Temple*; Lesslie Newbigin, *The Household of God*; Stanley Hauerwas and William H. Willimon, *Resident Aliens*; John Howard Yoder, *The Royal Priesthood*; George Eldon Ladd, *Gospel of the Kingdom* and *The Presence of the Future*.
12. Peterson, 80.
13. Schweizer, 70.
14. Manson, *Jesus and the Christian*, 148.
15. H. R. Mackintosh, *The Christian Experience of Forgiveness*, 120.
16. Samuel Bolton, *The True Bounds of Christian Freedom*, 23.
17. Mackintosh, 148–149.
18. Hendry, 133.
19. Hulse, 57.
20. Francis Schaeffer, *True Spirituality*, 92.

21. Abraham Booth, *The Reign of Grace*, 122.
22. R. C. Sproul, *Faith Alone*, 144.
23. David Peterson, *Engaging with God*, 234.
24. E. F. Scott, *The Kingdom and the Messiah*, 90.
25. Peterson, *Engaging with God*, 213.
26. Manson, *Jesus and the Christian*, 195.
27. Bonhoeffer, 83.
28. Peterson, *Engaging with God*, 253.
29. James P. Hanigan, "Conscience and the Holy Spirit," in *Conscience*, 184.
30. Fee, 804.
31. Schweizer, 88.
32. Fee, 607.
33. Ibid., 419.
34. Torrance, 55.
35. Yoder, *The Royal Priesthood*, 62.
36. Hauerwas and Willimon, 83.
37. Peterson, *Engaging with God*, 198.
38. Ibid., 205.

CHAPTER 7

An Invitation to Live by Love

Where Do We Go from Here?

1. Tullian Tchividjian, *Surprised by Grace*, 149.
2. Goguel, 314.
3. Bender, 84.
4. Dietrich Bonhoeffer, *Ethics*, 94.
5. Nouwen, 107.
6. Kreeft, 157.

7. Ortberg, *The Me I Want to Be*, 202.

8. Newbigin, *The Gospel in a Pluralist Society*, 232–233.

9. Richard B. Hays, *The Moral Vision of the New Testament*, 375.

10. Wright, *The Challenge of Easter*, 44–45.

11. Louis H. Evans, Jr., *Hebrews*, 130.

12. Theodore H. Robinson, *The Epistle to the Hebrews*, 69–70. Reproduced by permission of Hodder and Stoughton Limited.